MASTER
KOREAN
GRAMMAR

LEVEL 2

TOMI KOREAN

MP3 Audio Material Download

 PDF Additional Workbook Download

To enhance your learning experience, audio material is available for download. Visit https://tomikorean.com/audios/ master-korean-grammar-level2. These audio resources are designed to complement your studies and improve your pronunciation and listening skills.

To download the workbook, please visit https://tomikorean.com/workbook-grammar-level2. The workbook provides extra exercises and practice materials to reinforce your understanding of Korean grammar concepts covered in the main textbook.

 Scan the QR code to visit the web page and access the audio files.

 Scan the QR code to visit the web page and access the pdf file.

For any inquiries or assistance, feel free to reach out to Tomi Korean at contact@tomikorean.com.

Copyright Notice

Introduction

Many Korean learners find learning the Korean language to be quite challenging due to its distinct structure, setting it apart from many other languages. Therefore, it is recommended to begin by familiarizing oneself with the basic grammar through learning and practice. We created this book to help you better understand basic Korean grammar. The following are the key aspects we focused on while developing this book:

- This Level 2 book, designed for upper beginners, contains 54 fundamental grammar points and about 470 basic words.

- This book allows you to gradually understand the complex rules of the Korean language by breaking them down into manageable units.

- The book is designed to help you internalize the rules through practice. Besides basic exercises for each unit, the book includes review tests at the end of each chapter and a workbook, which is available for free download from our website.

- The ultimate goal of mastering grammar is to use it proficiently in spoken and written Korean. This book is structured to facilitate the practical application of learned grammar in real-life situations.

Whether you've already acquired some knowledge of Korean or are new to it, this book will assist you in systematically organizing your learning. If you're a beginner, I believe this book will serve as the ideal starting point for your Korean learning journey, helping you build the essential foundation of the Korean language.

I sincerely hope that this book will be a valuable guide in your Korean learning journey.

April 2024,
Tomi Korean

How to use this book

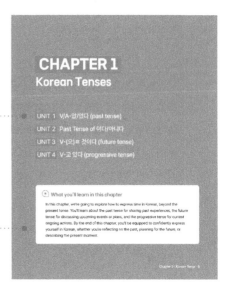

Unit Overview

To make it easier to understand essential grammar principles, the grammar topics have been systematically organized into units.

What to Expect in This Chapter

Preview the grammar concepts you will cover in this chapter.

Audio Resources

Listen to example sentences and exercises, and practice speaking using MP3 files downloaded from tomikorean.com.

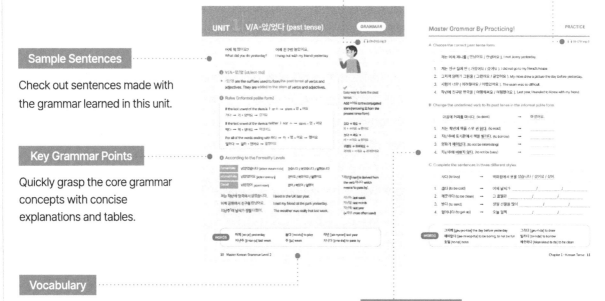

Sample Sentences

Check out sentences made with the grammar learned in this unit.

Key Grammar Points

Quickly grasp the core grammar concepts with concise explanations and tables.

Vocabulary

See newly introduced vocabulary at a glance.

Practice Session

Strengthen your understanding of the grammar from each unit by solving exercises.

Chapter Recap

Summarize and reinforce the key grammar points covered in each chapter.

Real-Life Conversation

Explore how the learned grammar is applied in authentic, everyday conversations.

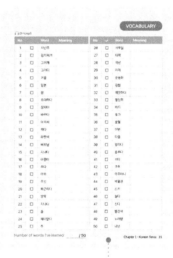

Vocabulary Checkpoint

Evaluate your mastery of new words introduced in each chapter through self-testing.

Review Test

Solidify your understanding of the essential grammar points through comprehensive review tests.

K-Culture Interlude

Finish each chapter with a short break, reading about Korean culture before moving to the next one.

Table of Contents

CHAPTER 1
Tenses

⊙ What you'll learn in this chapter

In this chapter, we're going to explore other tenses of Korean besides the present tense. You'll learn about the past tense for sharing past experiences, the future tense for discussing upcoming events or plans, and the progressive tense for current ongoing actions. By the end of this chapter, you'll be equipped to confidently express yourself in Korean, whether you're reflecting on the past, planning for the future, or describing the present moment.

UNIT | A/V-았/었다 (Past Tense)

🎧 01-01G.mp3

어제 뭐 했어요?
What did you do yesterday?

어제 친구랑 놀았어요.
I hung out with my friend yesterday.

❶ A/V-았/었 [at/eot]

▶ -았/었 are the suffixes used to form the past tense of verbs and adjectives. They are added to the stem of verbs and adjectives.

❷ Rules (informal polite form)

> If the last vowel of the stem is ㅏ or ㅗ → Stem + 았 + 어요
>
> 가다 → 가 + 았어요 → 갔어요
>
> If the last vowel of the stem is neither ㅏ nor ㅗ → Stem + 었 + 어요
>
> 먹다 → 먹 + 었어요 → 먹었어요
>
> For all of the words ending with 하다 → 하 + 였 + 어요 → 했어요
>
> 일하다 → 일하 + 였어요 → 일했어요

❸ Conjugation According to the Formality Levels

Formal Polite	A/V았/었습니다 [at/eot·sseum·ni·da]	갔습니다 / 먹었습니다 / 일했습니다
Informal Polite	A/V았/었어요 [at/eot·sseo·yo]	갔어요 / 먹었어요 / 일했어요
Casual	A/V았/었어 [at/eot·sseo]	갔어 / 먹었어 / 일했어

저는 작년에 영국에서 살았습니다.   I lived in the UK last year.

어제 공원에서 친구를 만났어요.   I met my friend at the park yesterday.

지난주[1]에 날씨가 정말 더웠어.   The weather was really hot last week.

✓ Easy way to form the past tense:

Add 써어요 to the conjugated stem (removing 요 from the present tense form). This applies whether the verb/adjective conjugates regularly or irregularly.

오다 → 와요 →
와 + 써어요 → 왔어요

쓰다 → 써요 →
써 + 써어요 → 썼어요

귀엽다 → 귀여워요 →
귀여워 + 써어요 → 귀여웠어요

[1] 지난 [ji·nan] is derived from the verb 지나다 which means 'to pass by'.

지난주: last week
지난달: last month
지난해: last year
(=작년: more often used)

WORDS

어제 [eo·je] yesterday	놀다 [nol·da] to play	작년 [jak·nyeon] last year
지난주 [ji·nan·ju] last week	주 [ju] week	지나다 [ji·na·da] to pass by

Master Grammar By Practicing!

 01-01P.mp3

A Choose the correct past tense form.

> 저는 어제 제니를 (만났어요 / 만넜어요). I met Jenny yesterday.

1. 저는 친구 집에 안 (가았어요 / 갔어요). I did not go to my friend's house.

2. 그저께 엄마가 그림을 (그렸어요 / 글었어요). My mom drew a picture the day before yesterday.

3. 시험이 너무 (어려웠어요 / 어렵었어요). The exam was so difficult.

4. 작년에 친구랑 한국을 (여행해써요 / 여행했어요). Last year, I traveled to Korea with my friend.

B Change the underlined verb to its past tense in the informal polite form.

> 아침에 커피를 <u>마시다</u>. (to drink) → <u>마셨어요.</u>

1. 저는 작년에 책을 스무 권 <u>읽다</u>. (to read) → _____

2. 지난주에 도서관에서 책을 <u>빌리다</u>. (to borrow) → _____

3. 영화가 <u>재미없다</u>. (to not be interesting) → _____

4. 지난주에 <u>바쁘지 않다</u>. (to not be busy) → _____

C Complete the sentence in three different styles.

> 사다 (to buy) → 백화점에서 옷을 <u>샀습니다 / 샀어요 / 샀어.</u>

1. 춥다 (to be cold) → 어제 날씨가 _____ / _____ / _____

2. 깨끗하다 (to be clean) → 그 호텔은 _____ / _____ / _____

3. 받다 (to receive) → 생일 선물을 많이 _____ / _____ / _____

4. 일어나다 (to get up) → 오늘 일찍 _____ / _____ / _____

WORDS

그저께 [geu·jeo·kke] the day before yesterday
재미없다 [jae·mi·eop·tta] to be boring, to not be fun
호텔 [ho·tel] hotel

그리다 [geu·ri·da] to draw
빌리다 [bil·li·da] to borrow
깨끗하다 [kkae·kkeut·ta·da] to be clean

🎧 01-02G.mp3

어제는 제 생일이었어요.
Yesterday was my birthday.

엄마는 가수가 아니었어요.
My mom was not a singer.

❶ N이었/였 [i·eot/yeot]

▶ The past tense of 이다 is formed by adding the suffixes -이었/였 to the noun.

❷ Rules (informal polite form)

> If the noun ends in a consonant → Noun + 이었 + 어요 → 이었어요
> 학생이다 → 학생 + 이었어요 → 학생이었어요
>
> If the noun ends in a vowel → Noun + 였 + 어요 → 였어요
> 가수다 → 가수 + 였어요 → 가수였어요

Formal Polite	N이었/였습니다 [i·eot/yeot·sseum·ni·da]	학생이었습니다/가수였습니다
Informal Polite	N이었/였어요 [i·eot/yeot·sseo·yo]	학생이었어요/가수였어요
Casual	N이었/였어 [i·eot/yeot·sseo]	학생이었어/가수였어

이곳은 서점이었습니다.   This was a bookstore.

어제 저녁은 김치찌개였어요.   The dinner was kimchi stew yesterday.

그 아저씨[1]가 우리 집주인이었어.   That man was our house owner.

✓

N이/가 아니었다
[i/ga a·ni·eot·tta]

The past tense of 이/가 아니다 is 이/가 아니었다.

그건 제 구두가 아니었어요.
Those were not my shoes.

그 사람은 일본 사람이 아니었어. That person was not Japanese.

[1] 아저씨 [a·jeo·ssi] refers to middle-aged men and 아줌마 [a·jum·ma] refers to middle-aged women. Be cautious using these terms for younger people; it can be seen as disrespectful.

WORDS

김치찌개 [kim·chi·jji·gae] kimchi stew   아저씨 [a·jeo·ssi] mister, sir

주인 [ju·in] owner, proprietor   구두 [gu·du] (formal) shoes   일본 [il·bon] Japan

아줌마 [a·jum·ma] (= 아주머니 [a·ju·meo·ni]) auntie, ma'am

Master Grammar By Practicing!

🎧 01-02P.mp3

A Choose the correct option.

저는 작년까지 (학생였어요 / 학생이었어요).	I was a student until last year.

1. 거기는 (박물관이었어요 / 박물관였어요).   That place was a museum.
2. 걔는 베트남 (사람였어 / 사람이었어).   He/She was Vietnamese.
3. 저는 어제까지 (휴가였어요 / 휴가이었어요).   I was on vacation until yesterday.
4. 저희 엄마는 (배우였습니다 / 배우이었습니다).   My mother was an actress.

B Change the underlined part to its past tense, as in the example.

저거 제 <u>자동차이다</u>.	→	<u>자동차였어요</u> / <u>자동차가 아니었어요</u>.

1. 그분은 <u>의사이다</u>.   →   _____ / _____
2. 여기는 제 <u>사무실이다</u>.   →   _____ / _____
3. 언니의 취미는 <u>피아노이다</u>.   →   _____ / _____
4. 제 생일은 <u>월요일이다</u>.   →   _____ / _____

C Change the underlined part into a correct past form, in case it is incorrect.

그 사람은 <u>회사원이 아니었습니다</u>. (correct / incorrect)	→	<u>회사원이 아니었습니다</u>.

1. 오늘 점심은 <u>김밥이었어요</u>. (correct / incorrect)   →   _____
2. 그 학교는 <u>대학교이 아니었어요</u>. (correct / incorrect)   →   _____
3. 지난주까지 <u>방학이였습니다</u>. (correct / incorrect)   →   _____
4. 그거 엄마 <u>우산이 아니었어</u>. (correct / incorrect)   →   _____

WORDS

박물관 [bak·mul·gwan] museum   베트남 [be·teu·nam] Vietnam
휴가 [hyu·ga] vacation   사무실 [sa·mu·sil] office
김밥 [gim·bap] gimbap (Korean rice roll)   방학 [bang·hak] school vacation

🎧 01-03G.mp3

내일 영화 볼 거예요?
Are you going to see a movie tomorrow?

저희는 내년에 한국을 여행할 거예요.
We will travel to Korea next year.

❶ V-(으)ㄹ 것이다 [-(eu)l geo·si·da]

▶ -(으)ㄹ 것이다 is used to express an action that will occur in the future.
It is usually used to express a scheduled event, plan, or intention.

❷ Rules (informal polite form)

> If the stem ends in a consonant   → Stem + 을 거예요[1]
> 먹다 (to eat)   → 먹 + 을 거예요 → 먹을 거예요
>
> If the stem ends in a vowel or ㄹ   → Stem + ㄹ 거예요[1]
> 가다 (to go)   → 가 + ㄹ 거예요 → 갈 거예요
> 알다 (to know)   → 알 + ㄹ 거예요 → 알 거예요[2]

Formal Polite	V(으)ㄹ 것입니다 [eul geo·sim·ni·da]	먹을 것입니다 / 갈 것입니다
Informal Polite	V(으)ㄹ 거예요 [eul kkeo·ye·yo][3]	먹을 거예요 / 갈 거예요
Casual	V(으)ㄹ 거야 [eul kkeo·ya][3]	먹을 거야 / 갈 거야

A: 이번 주말에 뭐 할 거야?   What will you do this weekend?

B: 언니랑 쇼핑을 할 거예요.   I will go shopping with my sister.

Irregular Verbs

ㄷ ending verbs   듣다 to listen → 들을 거예요

ㅂ ending verbs   돕다 to help → 도울 거예요

엄마 말을 잘 들을 거예요.   I will listen to my mom's words well.

내일 친구 일을 도울 거예요.   I will help my friend with work tomorrow.

[1] (으)ㄹ 거예요 is a shortened form of (으)ㄹ 것이에요. The shortened form is commonly used.

[2] One ㄹ is omitted.
살다 (to live) → 살 거예요
열다 (to open) → 열 거예요

[3] 거예요 is pronounced as 꺼예요 [kkeo·ye·yo].

✓
Future tense can be expressed with -(으)ㄹ게요 and -겠다, often used for intentions or promises. You'll learn more in Chapter 6.

WORDS   내년 [nae·nyeon] next year   이번 [i·beon] this time, this   다음 [da·eum] next

Master Grammar By Practicing!

🎧 01-03P.mp3

A Choose the correct option.

저는 내일 한국어를 (공부할 거예요 / 공부하을 거예요).	I will study Korean tomorrow.

1. 우리는 함께 저녁을 (먹을 거야 / 멀 거야). 　　　We will have dinner together.

2. 내일 노래방에서 노래를 (부를 거예요 / 부으을 거예요). 　I will sing songs at the karaoke tomorrow.

3. 저는 오늘 집에서 엄마를 (돕을 거예요 / 도울 거예요). 　I will help my mom at home today.

4. 저희 엄마가 BTS 콘서트에 (갈 거예요 / 가 거예요). 　My mom will go to the BTS concert.

B Change the underlined verb to its future tense in the informal polite form.

내일은 아침 일찍 일어나다.	→	일어날 거예요.

1. 이번 주말에 친구를 초대하다. 　→ _____

2. 친구에게 편지를 쓰다. 　→ _____

3. 저는 이 옷을 바꾸다. 　→ _____

4. 내년부터 한국에서 살다. 　→ _____

C Complete the sentence in three different styles.

가다 (to go)	→	언니는 내년에 대학에 갈 것입니다 / 갈 거예요 / 갈 거야.

1. 퇴근하다 (to leave work) → 오늘 일찍 _____ / _____ / _____

2. 찍다 (to take a photo) → 내일 가족 사진을 _____ / _____ / _____

3. 타다 (to ride) → 겨울에 스키를 _____ / _____ / _____

4. 돕다 (to help) → 친구가 할머니를 _____ / _____ / _____

WORDS

노래방 [no·rae·bang] karaoke　　　초대하다 [cho·dae·ha·da] to invite　　바꾸다 [ba·kku·da] to change
대학 [dae·hak] university　　　　　퇴근하다 [toe·geun·ha·da] to leave work
찍다 [jjik·tta] to take a photo　　　겨울 [gyeo·ul] winter　　　　　스키 [seu·ki] ski

01-04G.mp3

아빠가 집에서 쉬고 있어요.
My dad is resting at home.

친구가 파란색 운동화를 신고 있어요.
My friend is wearing blue sneakers.

❶ V-고 있다 [-go it·tta]: **be V-ing**

▶ -고 있다 is used to indicate the present progressive tense.

▶ -고 있다 is added to the stem, regardless of its ending consonant or vowel.

▶ -고 있었다 is used to express an action that was ongoing in the past.

❷ Rules (informal polite form)

Present Progressive Tense	Past Progressive Tense
Stem + 고 있어요	Stem + 고 있었어요
먹다 → 먹고 있어요	먹다 → 머고 있었어요
자다 → 자고 있어요	자다 → 자고 있었어요

A: 제니 씨, 지금 뭐 하고 있어요?   Jenny, what are you doing now?

B: 지금 영화 보고 있어요.   I am watching a movie now.

A: 아까 어디에 있었어요?   Where were you a while ago?

B: 서점에서 책 사고 있었어요.   I was buying books at the bookstore.

❸ -고 있다 used with verbs[1] related to putting on or taking off

▶ -고 있다 indicates that the action's result is ongoing up to the present.

제니가 빨간색 바지를 입고 있어요.   Jenny is wearing red pants.

엄마가 모자를 쓰고 있어요.   My mom is wearing a hat.

✓

Conjugation according to the Formality Levels

Formal polite
V고 있습니다
먹다 → 먹고 있습니다

Informal polite
V고 있어요
먹다 → 먹고 있어요

Casual
V고 있어
먹다 → 먹고 있어

[1]입다 [ip·tta]
→ to wear (clothes)
신다 [sin·tta]
→ to wear (shoes)
쓰다 [sseu·da]
→ to wear (hat)

WORDS

파란색 [pa·ran·saek] blue   운동화 [un·dong·hwa] sneakers, sports shoes
아까 [a·kka] (a little) while ago   빨간색 [ppal·gan·saek] red   바지 [ba·ji] pants
쓰다 [sseu·da] to wear (hat)   신다 [sin·tta] to wear (shoes)

Master Grammar By Practicing!

 01-04P.mp3

A Choose the correct progressive form that matches the given tense.

아이가 춤을 <u>추다</u>. (present)	→	(추고 있어요 / 추고 있었어요)

1. 저는 아까 잠을 <u>자다</u>. (past) → (자고 있어요 / 자고 있었어요)
2. 엄마가 부엌에서 <u>요리하다</u>. (present) → (요리고 있어요 / 요리하고 있어요)
3. 도서관에서 책을 <u>읽다</u>. (present) → (읽고 있어요 / 읽고 있었어요)
4. 할머니가 드라마를 <u>보다</u>. (past) → (보고 있었어요 / 볼고 있었어요)

B Change the underlined verb to its progressive form in both present and past tense.

강아지가 집으로 <u>가다</u>.	→	<u>가고 있어요 / 가고 있었어요</u>

1. 저는 열심히 <u>공부하다</u>. → _____ / _____
2. 아이들이 공원에서 <u>놀다</u>. → _____ / _____
3. 가수가 노래를 <u>부르다</u>. → _____ / _____
4. 고양이가 우유랑 빵을 <u>먹다</u>. → _____ / _____

C Change the underlined part into a correct present progressive form.

언니가 파란색 구두를 <u>신으고 있어</u>. (correct / incorrect)	→ <u>신고 있어</u>

1. 오빠가 자전거를 <u>타아고 있어요</u>. (correct / incorrect) → _____
2. 아기가 <u>안 자고 있어요</u>. (correct / incorrect) → _____
3. 카페에서 저를 <u>기다려고 있었어요</u>? (correct / incorrect) → _____
4. 지금 음악을 <u>들고 있습니다</u>. (correct / incorrect) → _____

🎧 01-C.mp3

민호: 제인 씨, 잘 지냈어요? Jane, how have you been?

제인: 네, 잘 지냈어요. 민호 씨는요? I've been good. And you?

민호: 저도 잘 지냈어요. I've been good, too.

지금 뭐 하고 있어요? What are you doing now?

제인: 한국어 공부하고 있어요. I'm studying Korean.

다음 주에 토픽 시험을 볼 거예요. I'm going to take a TOPIK test next week.

민호: 아, 진짜요? 공부 많이 했어요? Oh, really? Have you been studying a lot?

제인: 아니요, 시간이 없었어요. No, I haven't had much time.

하지만 열심히 하고 있어요. But I'm studying hard.

민호: 제인 씨는 잘 할 거예요. 화이팅! You'll do great. You can do it!

✏️ 잘 지내다 literally means 'to live well'. In a greeting context, it's used to ask someone if he/she is doing well.

✏️ 화이팅! is a common Korean expression of encouragement, support, or motivation, derived from the English word 'fighting'. It is similar to saying 'You can do it!' or 'Good luck!' in English.

WORDS 지내다 [ji·nae·da] to live, to spend one's time

RECAP CHAPTER 1

❶ V/A-았/었 (Past Tense)

If the last vowel of the stem is ㅏ or ㅗ → stem + 았어요

If the last vowel of the stem is neither ㅏ nor ㅗ → stem + 었어요

Every verb with 하다 → 하다 changes to 했어요

Statement	Question
V-았어요 / V-었어요 / 했어요	V-았어요? / V-었어요? / 했어요?
갔어요 / 먹었어요 / 일했어요	갔어요? / 먹었어요? / 일했어요?

❷ Past Tense of 이다/아니다

If the noun ends in a consonant → N + 이었어요

If the noun ends with a vowel → N + 였어요

Statement	Question
N이었어요 / N였어요	N이었어요? / N였어요?
학생이었어요 / 가수였어요	학생이었어요? / 가수였어요?

❸ V-(으)ㄹ 것이다 (Future Tense)

If the stem ends in a consonant → stem + 을 거예요

If the stem ends with a vowel → stem + ㄹ 거예요

Statement	Question
V-을 거예요 / V-ㄹ 거예요	V-을 거예요? / V-ㄹ 거예요?
먹을 거예요 / 갈 거예요	먹을 거예요? / 갈 거예요?

❹ V-고 있다 (Progressive Tense)

Present progressive tense: verb stem + 고 있어요

Statement	Question
V-고 있어요	V-고 있어요?
먹고 있어요 / 가고 있어요	먹고 있어요? / 가고 있어요?

REVIEW TEST CHAPTER 1

A Choose the option that **incorrectly** matches the verb with its past tense.

① 마시다 - 마셨어요 ② 놀다 - 놀았어요

③ 춥다 - 춥었어요 ④ 깨끗하다 - 깨끗했어요

B Choose the option that is paired with the correct answers.

> 한나는 독일에서 선생님_____.
>
> 그거 제 자동차_____.

① 이었어요 - 였어요 ② 이었어요 - 이었어요

③ 였어요 - 이었어요 ④ 였어요 - 였어요

C Choose the correct future tense form of the underlined verb.

> 도서관에서 책을 빌리다.
>
> 한국어 팟캐스트를 듣다.

① 빌릴 거예요 - 들을 거예요

② 빌릴 거예요 - 들을 거예요

③ 빌렬 거예요 - 듣을 거예요

④ 빌렬 거예요 - 들을 거예요

D Choose the **incorrect** sentence.

① (일하다) 어디에서 일하고 있어요?

② (먹다) 어디에서 밥 먹고 있어요?

③ (걷다) 누구랑 같이 걸고 있었어요?

④ (공부하다) 무슨 공부하고 있었어요?

E In the following passage, choose the option that is written **incorrectly**.

> 저는 지난 주말에 친구를 ①만나었어요.
> 우리는 영화관에서 영화를 ②봤어요. 영화는
> ③재미없었어요. 그런데 여자 배우가 정말
> ④예뻤어요.

F Choose the option that is grammatically **incorrect** for the blank space.

> 제니: 마리아 씨는 _____이었어요?
>
> 마리아: 아니요, 저는 _____이 아니었어요.

① 대학생 ② 선생님

③ 배우 ④ 회사원

G Read the following dialogue and choose the **incorrect** statement.

> 수지: 민호 씨, 뭐 해요?
>
> 민호: 제니 생일 선물을 고르고 있어요.
>   수지 씨는 무슨 선물 할 거예요?
>
> 수지: 제니가 생일 파티 해요?
>
> 민호: 네, 내일 할 거예요. 몰랐어요?
>
> 수지: 제니가 저는 초대 안 했어요.
>
> 민호: 진짜요? 제니가 전화할 거예요.
>
> 수지: 그런데 저는 내일 시간 없어요.

① 민호는 제니의 선물을 고르고 있습니다.

② 내일 제니가 생일 파티를 합니다.

③ 제니는 수지를 초대하지 않았습니다.

④ 수지는 제니의 생일 파티에 갈 것입니다.

🎧 01-V.mp3

No.	✓	Word	Meaning	No.	✓	Word	Meaning
1	☐	구두		26	☐	신다	
2	☐	일본		27	☐	초대하다	
3	☐	어제		28	☐	바꾸다	
4	☐	아까		29	☐	빌리다	
5	☐	이번		30	☐	방학	
6	☐	깨끗하다		31	☐	김밥	
7	☐	주		32	☐	다음	
8	☐	지나다		33	☐	잠	
9	☐	호텔		34	☐	작년	
10	☐	휴가		35	☐	주인	
11	☐	아주머니		36	☐	놀다	
12	☐	겨울		37	☐	그저께	
13	☐	빨간색		38	☐	춤	
14	☐	대학		39	☐	내년	
15	☐	열심히		40	☐	파란색	
16	☐	지내다		41	☐	박물관	
17	☐	노래방		42	☐	그리다	
18	☐	잠자다		43	☐	아줌마	
19	☐	스키		44	☐	찍다	
20	☐	재미없다		45	☐	추다	
21	☐	아저씨		46	☐	퇴근하다	
22	☐	운동화		47	☐	김치찌개	
23	☐	사무실		48	☐	베트남	
24	☐	지난주		49	☐	춤추다	
25	☐	바지		50	☐	쓰다	

Number of words I've learned: _____ / 50

Exploring the Dangun Myth: The Founding Story of Korea

The Dangun myth is the founding myth of Korea and one of the most important myths for Koreans. Let's explore this fascinating story.

Long ago, Hwanin(환인)'s son, Hwanung(환웅), looked down at the human world from heaven and desired to rule a kingdom. Hwanung descended to the top of Mount Taebaek with 3,000 followers to oversee 360 tasks related to human life and civilization.

At that time, a bear and a tiger shared the same cave, longing to become human. Hwanung gave them a bundle of mugwort and twenty cloves of garlic, saying, "If you eat only this and endure not seeing sunlight for one hundred days, you will become human."

While the bear persevered and transformed into a woman after 21 days, the tiger could not endure and left the cave, thus failing to become human. The transformed bear-woman, Ungnyeo(웅녀), prayed to give birth. Emperor Hwanung, moved by her plea, temporarily assumed human form, married her, and they bore a son named Dangun Wanggeom(단군 왕검).

In 2333 BC, Dangun Wanggeom established the kingdom of Gojoseon(고조선) and ruled for 1,500 years before relocating the capital to Asadal on Mount Baekdu. He ruled the country peacefully until he ascended as a mountain deity in Asadal, reportedly at the age of 1,908.

The Dangun myth plays a crucial role in shaping the national spirit and historical identity of Koreans, with many regarding Dangun as their ancestor. For this reason, Dangun is considered a highly significant figure among Koreans.

October 3rd is celebrated as National Foundation Day in Korea, commemorating the day when Dangun descended from heaven and established the first kingdom, Gojoseon. This day is known as 개천절(Gaecheonjeol) meaning 'the day the sky opened'.

CHAPTER 2
Advanced Particles

⊙ What you'll learn in this chapter

After mastering the basic particles in Level 1, you're now ready to explore particles that will help you express comparisons, frequency, quantity, exclusivity, choice, and direction with precision and nuance. These particles are key in everyday Korean, allowing you to convey detailed and specific information. By the end of this chapter, you'll have a stronger grasp of how to express detailed thoughts, and sharpen your conversational skills in Korean.

02-01G.mp3

이 음식은 사탕처럼 달아요
This food is as sweet as candy.

아빠는 아이같이 웃었어요.
My dad laughed like a child.

❶ N처럼 [cheo·reom], **N같이** [ga·chi] : **like, as … as**

▶ 처럼 and 같이[1] are particles used to convey the idea that an action, situation, or characteristic is similar to the preceding noun.

[1]처럼 and 같이 are interchangeable.

❷ Rules

It's irrelevant whether the noun ends in a consonant or a vowel		
Noun + 처럼	**Noun + 같이**	
강아지처럼	강아지같이	like a puppy
한국 사람처럼	한국 사람같이	like a Korean

아이가 강아지처럼 걸어요. = 아이가 강아지같이 걸어요.

The child walks like a puppy.

다니엘은 한국 사람처럼 한국어를 잘해요.

= 다니엘은 한국 사람같이 한국어를 잘해요.

Daniel speaks Korean well like a Korean.

⚠ 같이 is also used as an adverb 'together', as learned in Level 1.

In this case, 같이 and 처럼 are not interchangeable.

저는 남자친구랑 같이 살아요.　　　I live with my boyfriend.

저는 남자친구랑 처럼 살아요. (X)

WORDS

사탕 [sa·tang] candy　　　달다 [dal·da] to be sweet

웃다 [ut·tta] to laugh　　　잘하다 [jal·ha·da] to do well, to be good (at)

Master Grammar By Practicing!

🎧 02-01P.mp3

A Choose the correct option.

> 민호는 미국 사람(처럼 / 하고) 영어를 잘해요.

1. 이 음식은 한국 음식(에서 / 같이) 매워요.

2. 사과가 케이크(이랑 / 처럼) 달아요.

3. 수지는 가수(같이 / 도) 노래를 잘 불러요.

4. 서울은 뉴욕(처럼 / 하고) 커요.

B Look at the picture and complete the sentences, using '처럼'.

0. 강아지　　　1. 산　　　2. 아빠　　　3. 물　　　4. 영화배우

> 아기가 <u>강아지처럼</u> 귀여워요.

1. 롯데타워는 _____ 높아요.　　　2. 제 남동생은 _____ 키가 커요.

3. 민호는 술을 _____ 마셔요.　　　4. 수지는 _____ 예뻐요.

C Choose the corresponding word and change the ending to '-아/어요' form.

달다　　　아름답다　　　울다　　　따뜻하다　　　친하다

> 여자친구가 아기처럼 <u>울어요</u>.

1. 날씨가 봄처럼 _____　　　2. 술이 주스처럼 _____

3. 한국의 산은 그림같이 _____　　　4. 우리는 가족같이 아주 _____

🎧 02-02G.mp3

기차가 한 시간마다 와요.
The train comes every hour.

한국에는 집집마다 김치 냉장고가 있어요.
In Korea, every home has a kimchi refrigerator.

❶ N마다 [ma·da]: **every, all**

▶ 마다 is a particle attached to a noun that expresses every or all, and it is used in two main ways.

✓ 마다 is attached to a noun regardless of whether the noun ends in a consonant or a vowel.

1) Indicating Regular Intervals: **마다** is used to signify that something occurs at regular time intervals or is a recurring event.

일주일마다 every week   한 시간마다 every hour

저희는 일주일마다 회의를 해요. We have meetings every week.

2) Indicating 'Every' or 'All': **마다** is used to describe a situation where something applies to every individual or entity within a group.

학생마다 each student   집집마다[1] in every house

방마다 에어컨이 있어요. There is an air conditioner in every room.

[1] 집집마다 is idiomatically used to mean every house or each house. However, you can also use 집마다.

❷ Comparing Frequency Expressions: –마다 vs. 매–

	with –마다	with 매–
every day	날마다 [nal·ma·da]	매일 [mae·il]
every week	일주일마다 [il·ju·il·ma·da]	매주 [mae·ju]
every month	달마다 [dal·ma·da]	매월/매달 [mae·wol/mae·dal]
every year	해마다 [hae·ma·da]	매년/매해 [mae·nyeon/mae·hae]

매– and –마다 are often interchangeable, but 매– is usually used for regular, routine events, while –마다 emphasizes each specific occurrence. Therefore, 매– is more common in everyday speech for its simplicity and habitual implication.[2]

[2] Examples:
저는 매일 운동해요.
I exercise every day.
저는 날마다 운동해요.
I exercise day by day.

WORDS

냉장고 [naeng·jang·go] refrigerator   회의 [hoe·ui] meeting
에어컨 [e·eo·keon] air conditioner

Master Grammar By Practicing!

🎧 02-02P.mp3

A Choose the option that corresponds to the given word.

(every day)	→	저는 (일주일마다 / 날마다) 한국어 공부를 해요.

1. (every five minutes) → 버스가 (오 분마다 / 십 분마다) 와요.
2. (every spring) → 우리 가족은 (여름마다 / 봄마다) 여행을 갔어.
3. (every friday) → 저는 (금요일마다 / 목요일마다) 피아노를 배워요.
4. (every two hours) → 엄마는 (세 시간마다 / 두 시간마다) 물을 마셔요.

B Fill in the blank with the appropriate word that corresponds to the given word.

every school (학교)	→	<u>학교마다</u> 학생 식당이 있어요.

1. every country (나라) → _____ 문화가 달라요.
2. every house (집) → _____ 자동차가 있어요.
3. every season (계절) → 한국은 _____ 날씨가 달라요.
4. every student (학생) → _____ 컴퓨터를 받았어요.

C Choose two appropriate words and write them in the blank.

일주일마다　　매주　　매년　　매월　　해마다　　날마다　　매일　　달마다

(every day)	→	저는 <u>매일 / 날마다</u> 수영을 해요.

1. (every year) → 저는 _____ 여름 방학에 고향에 가요.
2. (every week) → 제니는 _____ 열 시간 아르바이트를 해요.
3. (every month) → 나는 _____ 미용실에 가.
4. (every day) → _____ 한국어 공부를 해요?

WORDS

여름 [yeo·reum] summer　　　　**문화** [mun·hwa] culture　　　　**계절** [gye·jeol] season
고향 [go·hyang] hometown　　　**미용실** [mi·yong·sil] beauty salon

02-03G.mp3

저는 매달 다섯 권쯤 책을 읽어요.
I read about five books every month.

오후 세 시 정도에 축구를 할 거야.
I will play soccer around 3 PM.

❶ N쯤 [jjeum] : about, around

▶ 쯤 is used to indicate an approximate amount, time, or degree. It's a way to convey that the speaker is giving a rough estimate.

▶ 쯤 is added after a noun, regardless of whether the noun ends in a consonant or a vowel.

열 명쯤 about ten people   오후 두 시쯤 around 2 PM

일주일에[1] 두 번[2]쯤 테니스를 쳐요. I play tennis about 2 times a week.

❷ N 정도 [jung·do] : about, around

▶ 정도 is used similarly to 쯤 to express an approximation or an estimate.

▶ 정도 is added after a noun with a space between the noun and 정도.

한 시간 정도 about an hour   한 달 정도 about a month

커피를 하루에 세 잔 정도 마셔요. I drink about three cups of coffee a day.

❸ Differences between N쯤 and N 정도

▶ 쯤 is more casual and often used in daily conversation, while 정도 is slightly more formal and used in both spoken and written Korean.[3]

▶ 쯤 is typically used with numbers, times, and quantities, whereas 정도 has a broader range of applications.

헨리의 한국어는 다섯 살 아이 정도예요.
Henry's Korean is about the level of a five-year-old child.

[1] N에 is used to specify the frequency of an action over a defined time period, indicating how often an activity occurs.
하루에 한 번 once a day
한달에 두 번 twice a month

[2] 번 is used with numbers to show how many times something happens, similar to the word "times" in English.
한 번: once
두 번: twice
세 번: tree times

[3] However, 쯤 and 정도 can be used interchangeably in most cases to indicate approximations.

WORDS

축구 [chuk·gu] soccer   테니스 [te·ni·seu] tennis
치다 [chi·da] to hit, to play   하루 [ha·ru] day, a day

Master Grammar By Practicing!

🎧 02-03P.mp3

A Fill in the blank using '쯤'.

A: 어제 몇 시에 잤어요? (열 시)	B: 어제 <u>열 시쯤</u>에 잤어요.

1. A: 물이 몇 병 있어요? (다섯 병)　　　　　 B: 물이 _____ 있어요.

2. A: 집에 언제 갔어요? (한 시)　　　　　　 B: 집에 _____ 갔어요.

3. A: 한국에 언제 갈 거예요? (내년 봄)　　　 B: 한국에 _____ 갈 거예요.

4. A: 서울에서 미국까지 비행기로 몇 시간 걸려요? (열두 시간)　 B: 비행기로 _____ 걸려요.

B Fill in the blank with the appropriate word that corresponds to the given word, using '정도'.

(three times)	→	일주일에 <u>세 번 정도</u> 운동해요.

1. (about 2 cups of coffee)　　 →　 커피를 하루에 _____ 마셔요.

2. (about 4 hours)　　　　　　 →　 부산까지 기차로 _____ 걸려요.

3. (around 20,000 won)　　　　 →　 이 운동화는 _____ 해요.

4. (about a week)　　　　　　 →　 지난주에 아팠어요. _____ 약을 먹었어요.

C Rewrite the underlined word by exchanging '쯤' with '정도' and '정도' with '쯤'.

나 어제 <u>두 시간쯤</u> 한국어 공부했어.	→	<u>두 시간 정도</u>

1. 한국어 수업은 보통 <u>다섯 시 정도</u>에 끝나요.　 →　 _____

2. 저 분은 <u>마흔 살쯤</u> 되었어요.　　　　　　 →　 _____

3. 회의는 <u>한 시간쯤</u> 걸릴 거예요.　　　　　 →　 _____

4. 이 케이크는 <u>만 원 정도</u> 해요.　　　　　　 →　 _____

WORDS

약 [yak] medicine　　　　　　　　**끝나다** [kkeut·na·da] to end

되다 [doe·da] to become　　　　　 **원** [won] won (Korean currency)

-쯤 하다 is used to indicate approximate prices.

UNIT 4 │ N밖에 (only, nothing but)

🎧 02-04G.mp3

기차가 오 분밖에 안 늦었어요.　　책상 위에 책밖에 없어요.
The train was only five minutes late.　　There is nothing but books on the desk.

❶ N밖에 [bak·kke] : only, nothing but

▶ 밖에 is used to emphasize the exclusivity of a noun, similar to the
meaning of only or nothing but in English.

▶ 밖에 is always used with negative verbs to convey the sense that
nothing else except for the mentioned noun is possible, available,
or exists in the context.

✓
밖에 is attached to a noun
regardless of whether the
noun ends in a consonant or
a vowel.

냉장고에 주스밖에 <u>없어요</u>. There is nothing but juice in the fridge.
냉장고에 주스밖에 있어요. (X)

저는 콜라밖에 <u>안 마셔요</u>. I drink nothing but cola.
저는 콜라밖에 마셔요. (X)

❷ Differences between N만 and N밖에

▶ Both 만 and 밖에 are translated as only in English. However, they differ
in usage and connotation.

▶ 만 is used in both positive and negative sentences[1], while
밖에 can be used in negative sentences only.

▶ 만 is more neutral or positive, indicating a choice, whereas
밖에 often conveys a negative connotation.
밖에 is often used when your expectations are not met.

[1] 만 can also be used in
negative sentence, but
it changes the meaning
significantly.
제 남편은 한국 음식만 안 먹어요.
My husband doesn't eat only
Korean food.
(He eats all the other food.
→ This is the opposite
meaning of 한국 음식만 먹어요.)

제 남편은 한국 음식만 먹어요. My husband eats only Korean food.
제 남편은 한국 음식밖에 안 먹어요. My husband eats only Korean food.
(It seems that the speaker doesn't like the fact.)

WORDS　　늦다 [neut·tta] to be late

Master Grammar By Practicing!

🎧 02-04P.mp3

A Choose the correct option.

> 나 어제 한 시간밖에 공부 (했어 / 못 했어).

1. 슈퍼마켓에서 소금밖에 (안 샀어요 / 샀어요).
2. 저는 운동 중에서 수영밖에 (해요 / 못 해요).
3. 이 방에는 침대밖에 (있어요 / 없어요).
4. 내 생일 파티에 친구가 세 명밖에 (안 왔어 / 왔어).

B Fill in the blank with the word that corresponds to the given word, using '만' or '밖에'.

> We only have cats in our house. (고양이) → 우리집에는 <u>고양이만</u> 있어요.

1. It took only four hours to Busan. (네 시간) → 부산까지 _____ 안 걸렸어요.
2. Jisoo listens to nothing but K-pop. (케이팝) → 지수는 _____ 안 들어요.
3. My brother only looks at his cellphone. (핸드폰) → 오빠는 집에서 _____ 봐요.
4. Among Korean foods, I only like kimbap. (김밥) → 저는 한국 음식 중에서 _____ 좋아해요.

C Correct the underlined word, in case it is incorrect.

> A: 누가 숙제를 했어요? B: 우리 반에서 제니밖에 숙제를 했어요. (correct / incorrect) → 제니만

1. A: 필통 안에 뭐가 있어요? B: 필통 안에 <u>지우개밖에</u> 있어요. (correct / incorrect) → _____
2. A: 냉장고에 아이스크림이 있어요? B: 아니요, <u>우유만</u> 없어요. (correct / incorrect) → _____
3. A: 필통 안에 연필이 많아요? B: 연필이 <u>한 개만</u> 없어요. (correct / incorrect) → _____
4. A: 선생님이 많이 늦었어요? B: <u>오 분밖에</u> 안 늦었어요. (correct / incorrect) → _____

WORDS

슈퍼마켓 [syu·peo·ma·ket] supermarket   소금 [so·geum] salt   반 [ban] class
숙제 [suk·je] homework   필통 [pil·tong] pencil case
지우개 [ji·u·gae] eraser   많다 [man·ta] to be a lot

UNIT 5 | N(이)나 ② (as much as)

02-05G.mp3

학교까지 한 시간이나 걸려요.   저희 집에 고양이가 세 마리나 있어요.
It takes as long as an hour to get to school.   We have as many as three cats in our house.

❶ N(이)나 ② [i·na] : as much as, no less than

▶ (이)나 is used to express that the number or amount of something is unexpectedly high or greater than expected, often conveying a sense of surprise or emphasis.

❷ Rules

If the noun ends in a consonant,	If the noun ends in a vowel,
Noun + 이나	**Noun + 나**
열 살이나 as old as ten years	열 개나 as many as ten

콜라를 다섯 병이나 마셨어요.[1] I drank as many as five bottles of cola.
돈이 천 달러나 있어요.[1] I have as much as a thousand dollars.

❸ N(이)나 ③ [i·na] : or something, just

▶ (이)나 is also used to express a casual, spontaneous decision or an action taken when there are no better alternatives, or simply for the sake of doing something.

냉장고에 고기가 없어요. 라면이나 먹을까요?[2]
There is no meat in the fridge. Shall we eat ramen or something?

심심해. 게임이나 하자.[2] I'm bored. Let's just play a game.

✓ Note that the (이)나 you are learning in this unit has a different usage from the (이)나 ① meaning 'or' that you learned in Level 1.

[1] If you use 밖에 in the negative form instead of (이)나, the perspective on the same situation becomes the opposite.

맥주를 다섯 병밖에 안 마셨어요.
I only drank five bottles of beer.
돈이 천 달러밖에 없어요.
I only have a thousand dollars.

[2] In this usage, (이)나 is commonly used in sentences that suggest, command, or request something. This sentence structure will be covered in Chapter 7.

WORDS
돈 [don] money
게임 [ge·im] game
심심하다 [sim·sim·ha·da] to be bored

Master Grammar By Practicing!

🎧 02-05P.mp3

A Choose the correct option.

> 지갑에 십 달러(나 / 이나) 있어요

1. 한국에서 이십 년(나 / 이나) 살았어요.

2. 가방에 책이 열 권(이나 / 나) 있어요.

3. 그 남자를 세 번(나 / 이나) 만났어요.

4. 오렌지를 서른 개(나 / 이나) 샀어요.

B Fill in the blank using '(이)나'.

> A: 강아지가 몇 마리 있어요? (5 dogs)　　　B: 강아지가 <u>다섯 마리나</u> 있어요.

1. A: 커피를 몇 잔 마셨어요? (3 cups of coffee)　　B: 커피를 _____ 마셨어요.

2. A: 오늘 몇 시간 운동했어요? (2 hours)　　B: _____ 운동했어요.

3. A: 지갑에 돈이 얼마 있어요? (50,000 won)　　B: 돈이 _____ 있어요.

4. A: 언니가 몇 살 많아요? (7 years older)　　B: 언니가 저보다 _____ 많아요.

C Fill in the blank with the appropriate word with '(이)나', considering the given word.

> (as many as 5 bottles) → 물을 <u>다섯 병이나</u> 마셨어요.

1. (as many as 20 people) → 파티에 손님이 _____ 왔어요.

2. (as long as 10 hours) → 오늘 회사에서 _____ 일했어.

3. (as many as 5 times) → 올해 _____ 여행을 했어요.

4. (as many as 8 books) → 도서관에서 책을 _____ 빌렸어요.

WORDS

지갑 [ji·gap] wallet　　　오렌지 [o·ren·ji] orange

얼마 [eol·ma] how much　　손님 [son·nim] customer

🎧 02-06G.mp3

엄마가 식탁에다가 꽃을 놓았어요.
Mom placed flowers on the table.

학교에서부터 집까지 걸었어요.
I walked from school to home.

❶ N에게로 [e·ge·ro]: **to, toward**

▶ 에게로 is used to indicate the movement towards a person.

▶ N에게 (particle indicating a person as the recipient or target) +
로 (adding directionality).

내일 여자친구에게로 갈 거예요. = 내일 여자친구에게[1] 갈 거예요.
I will go to my girlfriend tomorrow.

[1] 에게로 can be replaced with 에게.
에게로 emphasizes direction by adding 로 to 에게, highlighting the directional aspect more distinctly.

❷ N에다가 [e·da·ga]: **in, on**

▶ 에다가 is used to add something to a specific place or object.

▶ N에 (particle indicating location) + 다가 (adding directionality).

커피에다가 우유를 조금 넣었어요. = 커피에[2] 우유를 조금 넣었어요.
I added a little milk to the coffee.

[2] 에다가 can be replaced with 에.

❸ N에서부터 [e·seo·bu·teo]: **from**

▶ 에서부터 is used to indicate the starting point of an action or range.

▶ N에서 (particle indicating the origin) + 부터 (emphasizing the beginning).

서울에서부터 부산까지 기차로 갔어요. = 서울에서[3] 부산까지 기차로 갔어요.
I went from Seoul to Busan by train.

월요일에서부터 시험을 봐요. = 월요일부터[3] 시험을 봐요.
I have exams starting from Monday.

[3] 에서부터 can be replaced with 에서 (locational) or 부터 (tamporal)

WORDS

식탁 [sik·tak] dining table   놓다 [no·ta] to place   넣다 [neo·ta] to put, to add

"놓다" is to place something on top of something, "넣다" is to insert something into something else.

Master Grammar By Practicing!

 02-06P.mp3

A Replace the underlined word with a word that emphasizes it more.

I am going towards my parents.	<u>부모님에게</u> 가고 있어요. → <u>부모님에게로</u>

1. I will hang a picture on the wall.　　　　<u>벽에</u> 그림을 걸 거예요. → _____

2. We will have a meeting starting from 10.　<u>10시부터</u> 회의를 할 거예요. → _____

3. I wrote a letter on the paper.　　　　　　<u>종이에</u> 편지를 썼어요. → _____

4. My friend brought a gift to me.　　　　　친구가 <u>저에게</u> 선물을 가져왔어요. → _____

B Choose the correct option.

책상 위(에서부터 / 에다가) 가방을 놓았어요.

1. 국(에다가 / 에게로) 소금을 너무 많이 넣었어요.

2. 아이가 엄마(에게로 / 에다가) 걸어갔어요.

3. 파티는 저녁 일곱 시(에서부터 / 에다가) 해요.

4. 여기(에다가 / 에서부터) 저기까지 몇 킬로미터예요?

C Choose the corresponding word and write it in the blank.

에게로　　　　　에다가　　　　　에서부터

가방<u>에다가</u> 책을 넣었어요.

1. 식당이 여섯 시_____ 열어요.

2. 저는 남자친구_____ 돌아가고 싶어요.

3. 지갑 안_____ 가족 사진을 넣었어요.

4. 회사_____ 우리집까지 너무 멀어요.

WORDS

걸다 [geol·da] to hang　　　　　종이 [jong·i] paper　　　　　가져오다 [ga·jyeo·o·da] to bring
킬로미터 [kil·lo·mi·teo] kilometer　걸어가다 [geo·reo·ga·da] to walk
국 [guk] soup　　　　　　　　　돌아오다 [do·ra·o·da] to come back

🎧 02-C.mp3

헨리: 수지 씨, 오랜만이에요. Suzy, long time no see.

수지: 안녕하세요! 헨리 씨 어디 가요? Hello! Where are you going?

헨리: 저 지금 수영장 가요. I'm going to the swimming pool now.

요즘 주말마다 수영하고 있어요. I've been swimming every weekend lately.

수지: 저도 일주일에 한 번 정도 수영장에 가요.
I also go to the swimming pool about once a week.

그런데 요즘 너무 바빴어요. But I've been too busy recently.

그래서 지난 달에는 한 번밖에 못 갔어요. So, I only went once last month.

헨리: 저는 매 주말마다 가고 있어요. I go there every weekend.

수지: 진짜요? 저도 헨리 씨처럼 매주 수영하고 싶어요!
Really? I also want to swim every week like you!

✏️ 오랜만이에요 is a Korean phrase meaning "long time no see" used when greeting someone you haven't seen in a while.

✏️ 매 translates to 'every' and 마다 also conveys a similar meaning of 'every'. When used together, as in '매 주말마다(every weekend)', it serves to emphasize the regularity and consistency of the event or action.

RECAP CHAPTER 2

❶ N처럼, N같이: like, as…as

Particles used to convey the idea that an action, situation, or characteristic is similar to the preceding noun, indicating the meaning of 'like'.

❷ N마다: every, all

1. **Indicating Regular Intervals:** Used to signify that something occurs at regular time intervals or is a recurring event.
2. **Indicating 'All':** Used to describe a situation where something applies to every individual.

❸ N쯤, N 정도: about, around

Particles used to express an approximation or an estimate.
1. 쯤: More casual and often used with numbers, time-related nouns, or quantities.
2. 정도: More formal and used in a broader range of contexts than 쯤.

❹ N밖에: only, nothing but

Particle used to emphasize the exclusivity of a noun, indicating the meaning of 'only' or 'nothing but'. It is always used in negative sentences.

❺ N(이)나: as much as

1. Used to express that the number or amount of something is greater than expected.
2. Used to express a spontaneous decision when there are no better alternatives.

If the noun ends in a consonant → N + 이나
If the noun ends in a vowel → N + 나

❻ N에게로:to, N에다가: in, on, N에서부터: from

1. 에게로: 에게 (indicating a person as the recipient) + 로 (adding directionality)
2. 에다가: 에 (indicating location) + 다가 (adding directionality)
3. 에서부터: 에서 (indicating the origin) + 부터 (emphasizing the beginning).

REVIEW TEST CHAPTER 2

A   Choose the particle that can commonly fill in the blanks.

> 서점에서 책을 다섯 권( ) 샀어요.
> 지갑에 이만 원( ) 있어요.

① 밖에   ② 쯤
③ 마다   ④ 에다가

B   Choose the correct sentence.

① 저는 술을 두 잔밖에 마셨어요.
② 잠을 네 시간밖에 잤어요
③ 작년에 영화를 다섯 개밖에 봤어요.
④ 저는 친구가 한 명밖에 없어요.

C   Choose the incorrect sentence.

① 노래를 두 시간이나 불렀어요.
② 냉장고에 콜라가 다섯 병이나 있어요.
③ 이 모자는 삼만 원나 해요.
④ 심심해요. 드라마나 봐요.

D   In the following passage, choose the option that is written incorrectly.

> 헨리는 ①가수처럼 노래를 잘 해요. 매일 ②한 시간 정도 노래를 불러요. 그리고 ③주말마다 노래방에 가요. 거기에서 ④세 시간밖에 노래 해요.

E   Choose the sentence where the underlined word is incorrect.

① 오빠가 벽에다가 그림을 걸어요.
② 아이가 아빠에게로 걸어가요.
③ 학교에서까지 너무 멀어요.
④ 침대에다가 옷을 놓았어요.

F   Choose the option that is grammatically correct for the blank space.

> 제니가 책을 다섯 권 _____ 읽었어요.
> 고양이가 네 마리 _____ 있어요.

① 이나 - 이나   ② 나 - 나
③ 나 - 이나   ④ 이나 - 나

G   Read the following dialogue and choose the incorrect statement.

> 유코: 지수 씨 어제 뭐 했어요?
> 지수: 저 어제 두 시쯤에 제니 만났어요.
>   다섯 시간이나 같이 쇼핑했어요.
> 유코: 뭐 샀어요?
> 지수: 저는 모자만 샀어요.
>   제니도 치마밖에 안 샀어요.
> 유코: 요즘 옷은 얼마 해요?
> 지수: 옷마다 달라요.
>   제 치마는 오만 원 정도 했어요.

① 지수는 어제 제니를 만났습니다.
② 지수와 제니는 다섯 시간쯤 쇼핑했습니다.
③ 제니는 치마를 사지 않았습니다.
④ 지수의 치마는 오만 원 정도였습니다.

🎧 02-V.mp3

No.	✓	Word	Meaning	No.	✓	Word	Meaning
1	☐	냉장고		26	☐	슈퍼마켓	
2	☐	놓다		27	☐	봄	
3	☐	넣다		28	☐	고향	
4	☐	계절		29	☐	되다	
5	☐	필통		30	☐	걸어가다	
6	☐	약		31	☐	많다	
7	☐	축구		32	☐	반	
8	☐	끝나다		33	☐	가져오다	
9	☐	손님		34	☐	걸다	
10	☐	지우개		35	☐	케이크	
11	☐	에어컨		36	☐	달다	
12	☐	여름		37	☐	지갑	
13	☐	사탕		38	☐	테니스	
14	☐	소금		39	☐	치다	
15	☐	심심하다		40	☐	회의	
16	☐	식탁		41	☐	울다	
17	☐	웃다		42	☐	게임	
18	☐	문화		43	☐	하루	
19	☐	미용실		44	☐	종이	
20	☐	잘하다		45	☐	숙제	
21	☐	국		46	☐	친하다	
22	☐	아름답다		47	☐	늦다	
23	☐	얼마		48	☐	원	
24	☐	돌아오다		49	☐	킬로미터	
25	☐	돈		50	☐	오렌지	

Number of words I've learned: _____ / 50

Symbols of South Korea's National Flag: 태극기 (Taegeukgi)

Do you know that the name of the South Korean national flag is 태극기(Taegeukgi)? Let's explore what each symbol on the Taegeukgi represents.

The Taegeukgi consists of a white background with a 태극(Taegeuk) symbol in the center and four trigrams of 건(Geon), 곤(Gon), 감(Gam), and 리(Ri) at the corners.

The white background of the Taegeukgi represents brightness, purity, and the nation's traditional love for peace. The Taegeuk symbol in the center symbolizes the harmony of Yin (blue) and Yang (red), embodying the truth of the universe where all things are created and developed through the interaction of Yin and Yang.

The Geon trigram at the upper left symbolizes the sky, the Gon trigram at the lower right symbolizes the earth, the Gam trigram at the upper right symbolizes water, and the Ri trigram at the lower left symbolizes fire. These four trigrams represent the unity and harmony of unification centered around the Taegeuk.

Derived from the Taegeuk pattern, which our ancestors have used in their daily lives since ancient times, the Taegeukgi embodies the ideal of the Korean people who continuously pursue creation and prosperity along with the universe.

While the Taegeukgi can be hoisted daily, it is typically raised on national holidays and major commemorative days:

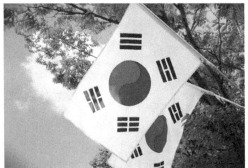

3.1절 (Independence Movement Day, March 1st)
현충일 (Memorial Day, June 6th)
제헌절 (Constitution Day, July 17th)
광복절 (Liberation Day, August 15th)
국군의 날 (Armed Forces Day, October 1st)
개천절 (National Foundation Day, October 3rd)
한글날 (Hangul Day, October 9th)

CHAPTER 3
Ability and Possibility

UNIT 1 V-(으)ㄹ 수 있다/없다 (can/cannot)

UNIT 2 V-(으)ㄹ 줄 알다/모르다 (to/to not know how to do)

◉ What you'll learn in this chapter

Chapter 3 focuses on expressing abilities and possibilities, expanding your Korean language skills to talk about what can be done and what someone knows how to do. This chapter equips you with the tools to discuss skills, abilities, and possibilities in various contexts, enhancing your conversational depth in Korean. By the end of this chapter, you'll be more adept at describing not just what happens, but also what might happen or what someone is capable of doing.

UNIT 1 | V-(으)ㄹ 수 있다/없다 (can/cannot)   GRAMMAR

🎧 03-01G.mp3

제니는 탁구를 칠 수 있어요.
Jenny can play table tennis.

이 컴퓨터를 쓸 수 있어요?
Can I use this computer?

❶ V-(으)ㄹ 수 있다/없다¹ [(eu)l su it·tta/eop·tta] : **can/cannot**

▶ (으)ㄹ 수 있다/없다 is used when someone is/is not able to do something, or when something is possible/impossible.

❷ Rules

If the stem ends in a consonant → Stem + 을 수 있다/없다	
먹다 (to eat) → 먹 + 을 수 있다/없다 → 먹을 수 있다/없다	
If the stem ends in a vowel or ㄹ¹ → Stem + ㄹ 수 있다/없다	
가다 (to go) → 가 + ㄹ 수 있다/없다 → 갈 수 있다/없다	
살다 (to live) → 살 + ㄹ 수 있다/없다 → 살 수 있다/없다²	

Formal Polite	V(으)ㄹ 수 있습니다 [eul su it·sseum·ni·da]	먹을 수 있습니다/갈 수 있습니다
Informal Polite	V(으)ㄹ 수 있어요 [eul su it·sseo·yo]	먹을 수 있어요/ 갈 수 있어요
Casual	V(으)ㄹ 수 있어 [eul su it·sseo]	먹을 수 있어/ 갈 수 있어

A: 무슨 외국어를 할 수 있어요?　What foreign language can you speak?
B: 독일어³를 할 수 있어요.　　　 I can speak German.

Irregular Verbs

ㄷ ending verbs　　　듣다 to listen → 들을 수 있어요/없어요

ㅂ ending verbs　　　돕다 to help → 도울 수 있어요/없어요

저는 지금 음악을 들을 수 없어요.　I cannot listen to music right now.
내가 숙제를 도울 수 있어.　　　　I can help with your homework.

---

¹V-(으)ㄹ 수 있다 is formed by adding -(으)ㄹ to the verb stem, combined with 수 meaning 'way' or 'method' and 있다.

² One ㄹ is omitted.
살을 수 있다/없다 (X)
열다 (to open) → 열 수 있다

³ Appending 어 to the name of a country transforms it into the name of the language spoken in that country.
일본어: Japanese
프랑스어: French

✓
The past tense form of (으)ㄹ 수 있어요/없어요 is (으)ㄹ 수 있었어요/없었어요.
집에 일찍 갈 수 없었어요.
I couldn't go home early.

WORDS　탁구 [tak·gu] table tennis　쓰다 [sseu·da] to use　외국어 [oe·gu·geo] foreign language

Master Grammar By Practicing!

🎧 03-01P.mp3

A Choose the correct option.

> 저는 한국어를 (할 수 있어요 / 하을 수 있어요).

1. 지금 2층에 (올라갈 수 없어요 / 올라가알 수 없어요).
2. 할머니가 핸드폰을 (쓸 수 있어요 / 쓰을 수 있어요).
3. 저는 독일어 책을 (읽수 있습니다 / 읽을 수 있습니다).
4. 문을 (닫을 수 없어? / 달을 수 없어?)

B Change the underlined verb to '-(으)ㄹ 수 있어요/없어요' form.

> 아침에 일찍 일어나다.   →   일어날 수 있어요 / 일어날 수 없어요

1. 다음주에 대사관에 가다.   →   _____ / _____
2. 남편이랑 잘 지내다.   →   _____ / _____
3. 저는 김밥을 만들다.   →   _____ / _____
4. 아이가 발을 씻다.   →   _____ / _____

C Fill in the blank to match the English sentence in informal polite form.

> I can dance. (춤을 추다)   →   저는 춤을 출 수 있어요.

1. Can I use the washing machine? (쓰다)   →   세탁기를 _____
2. I can send an email tonight. (보내다)   →   오늘 밤에 이메일을 _____
3. I couldn't use a card at the store. (쓰다)   →   가게에서 카드를 _____
4. I can sell things on the internet. (팔다)   →   인터넷으로 물건을 _____

WORDS

층 [cheung] floor (level)	올라가다 [ol·la·ga·da] to go up	인터넷 [in·teo·net] internet
문 [mun] door	대사관 [dae·sa·gwan] embassy	발 [bal] foot
세탁기 [se·tak·gi] washing machine	카드 [ka·deu] card	물건 [mul·geon] item

🎧 03-02G.mp3

엄마는 컴퓨터를 사용할 줄 알아요.　　저는 피아노를 칠 줄 몰라요.
My mom knows how to use a computer.　　I don't know how to play the piano.

❶ V-(으)ㄹ 줄 알다/모르다¹ [(eu)l jul al·da/mo·reu·da]

▶ (으)ㄹ 줄 알다 is used to express one's abilities in various skills.

▶ (으)ㄹ 줄 모르다 is used to express one's lack of abilities in skills.

❷ Rules

If the stem ends in a consonant → Stem + 을 줄 알다/모르다	
읽다 (to read) → 읽 + 을 줄 알다/모르다 → 읽을 줄 알다/모르다	
If the stem ends in a vowel or ㄹ → Stem + ㄹ 줄 알다/모르다	
쓰다 (to write) → 쓰 + ㄹ 줄 알다/모르다 → 쓸 줄 알다/모르다	
만들다 (to make) → 만들 + ㄹ 줄 알다/모르다 → 만들 줄 알다/모르다²	

저는 영어 책을 읽을 줄 알아요.　　I know how to read English books.

산드라는 한글을 쓸 줄 알아요.　　Sandra knows how to write Hangul.

¹줄: Used to represent the idea of 'way of doing'.
알다: to know
Formality level:
압니다, 알아요, 알아
모르다: to not know
Formality level:
모릅니다, 몰라요, 몰라

² One ㄹ is omitted.
만들을 줄 알아요 (X)
저는 불고기를 만들 줄 알아요.
I know how to make bulgogi.

Irregular conjugation for verbs ending in ㄷ and ㅂ

듣다 → 들을 줄 알아요/몰라요
굽다 → 구울 줄 알아요/몰라요

저는 케이크를 구울 줄 알아요.
I know how to bake a cake.

WORDS
사용하다 [sa·yong·ha·da] to use
불고기 [bul·go·gi] bulgogi (Korean BBQ)
한글 [han·geul] Hangul (Korean script)
굽다 [gup·tta] to grill, to bake

Master Grammar By Practicing!

🎧 03-02P.mp3

A Choose the correct option.

> 저는 운전을 (할 주를 알아요 / 할 줄 알아요).

1. 아이가 글을 (쓸 줄 압니다 / 쓰을 줄 압니다).
2. 우리 딸은 벌써 자전거를 (타알 줄 알아 / 탈 줄 알아).
3. 엄마는 한국 음식을 (먹을 줄 몰라요 / 먹를 줄 몰라요).
4. 떡볶이를 (만들 줄 알아요? / 만들을 줄 알아요?)

B Change the underlined verb to '-(으)ㄹ 줄 알아요/몰라요' form.

> 저는 테니스를 <u>치다</u>.　　　　→　　<u>칠 줄 알아요 / 칠 줄 몰라요</u>

1. 지수는 미국 사람처럼 영어를 <u>말하다</u>.　→　_____ / _____
2. 저는 비빔밥을 <u>만들다</u>.　→　_____ / _____
3. 다니엘은 야구를 <u>하다</u>.　→　_____ / _____
4. 동생은 사진을 <u>찍다</u>.　→　_____ / _____

C Fill in the blank to match the English sentence.

> I can swim. (수영을 하다)　　→　　저는 <u>수영을 할 줄 알아요</u>.

1. I don't know how to smoke cigarette. (담배를 피우다) → 저는 _____
2. My dad doesn't know how to grill meat. (고기를 굽다) → 아빠는 _____
3. Do you know how to speak Chinese? (중국어를 하다) → _____
4. My mom knows how to make Hanbok? (한복을 만들다) → 엄마는 _____

WORDS

글 [geul] writing　　　　　　벌써 [beol·sseo] already　　　　야구 [ya·gu] baseball
담배 [dam·bae] cigarette　　피우다 [pi·u·da] to smoke
한복 [han·bok] traditional Korean clothing

🎧 03-C.mp3

요코: 지은 씨, 지금 시간 있어요? Jieun, do you have time now?

지은: 네, 괜찮아요. 무슨 일이에요? Yes, it's okay. What's up?

요코: 지은 씨 케이크 만들 줄 알아요? Do you know how to make cakes?

지은: 네, 만들 수 있어요. Yes, I can make them.

요코: 친구한테 생일 케이크를 주고 싶어요. I wanna give a birthday cake to my friend.

그런데 저는 케이크 만들 줄 몰라요. But I don't know how to make one.

지은 씨가 도와줄 수 있어요? Can you please help me?

지은: 네, 그런데 오늘은 시간이 없어요. Yes, but I don't have time today.

내일은 어때요? 내일 가르쳐줄 수 있어요.
How about tomorrow? I can teach you then.

요코: 네, 좋아요! 정말 고마워요! Yes, that sounds great! Thank you so much!

✏️ 괜찮아요 translates to "It's okay" or "I'm fine" in English. It's often used to reassure someone that everything is alright or to politely decline an offer.

✏️ In the phrase 무슨 일이에요?, 일 means 'something' or 'matter', asking "What's the matter?" It's used to express concern ("What's wrong?") or casually inquire ("What's up?" or "What's going on?").

✏️ 어때요? can be translated as "How is it?" or "What do you think?" in English. It's used to ask for someone's opinion or to inquire about their feelings regarding something.

RECAP CHAPTER 3

❶ V-(으)ㄹ 수 있다/ 없다 (can/cannot)

If the stem ends in a consonant → stem + 을 수 있다/없다
If the stem ends in a vowel or ㄹ → stem + ㄹ 수 있다/없다

	Statement	Question
-(으)ㄹ 수 있다 can	V-을 수 있어요 / V-ㄹ 수 있어요 읽을 수 있어요 / 갈 수 있어요	V-을 수 있어요? / V-ㄹ 수 있어요? 읽을 수 있어요? / 갈 수 있어요?
-(으)ㄹ 수 없다 cannot	V-을 수 없어요 / V-ㄹ 수 없어요 읽을 수 없어요 / 갈 수 없어요	V-을 수 없어요? / V-ㄹ 수 없어요? 읽을 수 없어요? / 갈 수 없어요?

❷ V-(으)ㄹ 줄 알다/ 모르다 (to/to not know how to do)

If the stem ends in a consonant → stem + 을 줄 알다/모르다
If the stem ends in a vowel or ㄹ → stem + ㄹ 줄 알다/모르다

	Statement	Question
-(으)ㄹ 줄 알다 to know how to do	V-을 줄 알아요 / V-ㄹ 줄 알아요 읽을 줄 알아요 / 쓸 줄 알아요	V-을 줄 알아요? / V-ㄹ 줄 알아요? 읽을 줄 알아요? / 쓸 줄 알아요?
-(으)ㄹ 줄 모르다 to not know how to do	V-을 줄 몰라요 / V-ㄹ 줄 몰라요 읽을 줄 몰라요 / 쓸 줄 몰라요	V-을 줄 몰라요? / V-ㄹ 줄 몰라요? 읽을 줄 몰라요? / 쓸 줄 몰라요?

REVIEW TEST CHAPTER 3

A Choose the option that is paired with the correct answers.

> 내일 대사관에 (　　　) 있어요.
> 문을 (　　　) 없어요.

① 갈 수 - 닫을 수　　② 갈 수 - 달 수

③ 가을 수 - 닫을 수　④ 가을 수 - 달 수

B Choose the correct sentence.

① 이 세탁기 쓰을 수 있어요?

② 내가 내일 너를 도울 수 있어.

③ 김치를 만들을 수 있어요.

④ 옷을 바꾸울 수 없어요.

C Choose the correct option transformed into the '(으)ㄹ 줄 알아요' form.

> 엄마는 영어를 하다.
> 아빠는 고기를 굽다.

① 핼 줄 알아요 - 구울 줄 알아요

② 할 줄 알아요 - 굽을 줄 알아요

③ 할 줄 알아요 - 구울 줄 알아요

④ 핼 줄 알아요 - 굽을 줄 알아요

D Choose the sentence that is **incorrectly** translated into Korean.

① I can't open the door. - 문을 열 수 없어요.

② I couldn't drink water. - 물을 마실 수 없어요.

③ I could buy a book. - 책을 살 수 있었어요.

④ I can borrow money. - 돈을 빌릴 수 있어요.

E Choose the option that does **not** match the picture.

① 저는 피아노를 칠 줄 알아요.

② 저는 자전거를 탈 줄 알아요.

③ 저는 요리할 줄 알아요.

④ 저는 축구를 할 줄 알아요.

F Read the following dialogue and choose the **incorrect** statement.

> 유나: 헨리 씨는 수영할 줄 알아요?
> 헨리: 네, 저는 학교에서 배웠어요.
> 　　　유나 씨는요?
> 유나: 저는 수영을 못 해요.
> 헨리: 그럼 무슨 운동 할 수 있어요?
> 유나: 저는 테니스 칠 수 있어요.
> 　　　그리고 스키도 탈 줄 알아요.
> 　　　겨울 방학마다 스키를 타요.
> 헨리: 한국은 어디에서 스키 탈 수 있어요?
> 유나: 강원도의 산에서 탈 수 있어요.

① 유나는 수영을 할 줄 모릅니다.

② 헨리는 스키를 탈 줄 모릅니다.

③ 유나는 겨울에 스키를 탑니다.

④ 강원도에서 스키를 탈 수 있습니다.

🎧 03-V.mp3

No.	✓	Word	Meaning
1	☐	문	
2	☐	사용하다	
3	☐	물건	
4	☐	한복	
5	☐	인터넷	
6	☐	층	
7	☐	야구	
8	☐	카드	
9	☐	한글	
10	☐	벌써	
11	☐	세탁기	
12	☐	탁구	
13	☐	대사관	
14	☐	올라가다	
15	☐	굽다	
16	☐	글	
17	☐	피우다	
18	☐	불고기	
19	☐	외국어	
20	☐	쓰다	
21	☐	담배	
22	☐	발	

Number of words I've learned: _____ / 22

Exploring the South Korean Education System

Curious about the South Korean education system? In Korea, education typically consists of kindergarten, elementary school, middle school, high school, and university. During the compulsory education period, students can receive education free of charge.

초등학교 Elementary school (6 years, compulsory)
As it is compulsory education, all education is provided completely free of charge. The norm is to enroll at the age of 5, but it is also possible to enroll at the age of 6 or 7.

중학교 Middle School (3 years, compulsory)
During this stage, students delve deeper into academic subjects while also preparing for a standardized test that determines admission to high schools. Usually, from this time onwards, students start wearing school uniforms and are subject to some restrictions on their attire and hairstyles.

고등학교 High School (3 years)
High school education provides separate tracks: general for college preparation and vocational for career training. The goal of many high school students is fixed on attending a good university. Admission to top universities is highly competitive, as students aim to excel in 수능 (the College Scholastic Ability Test) to secure spots.

The academic year in all schools typically begins in March and ends in February of the following year, with summer vacation in July and August and winter vacation in December and January. After completing the academic year in February of the following year, students graduate or move up to the next grade.

CHAPTER 4
Honorific Expressions

UNIT 1 A/V-(으)시 (Honorific Suffix)

UNIT 2 N께서, N께서는, N께 (Honorific Particles)

UNIT 3 Special Honorific Words

What you'll learn in this chapter

You've learned about the Korean speech styles according to the formality level. In this chapter, we delve into other honorific forms. Understanding these forms is essential for communicating appropriately based on age, social status, and the degree of intimacy. You'll learn to apply honorific suffixes and particles, as well as special honorific terms. Mastering these elements enables you to navigate social situations more effectively, demonstrating the appropriate respect and consideration that are key in Korean society.

04-01G.mp3

선생님이 영어를 가르치세요.
The teacher teaches English.

할머니가 일본을 여행하셨어요.
My grandmother traveled to Japan.

❶ A/V-(으)시 [(eu)·si]

▶ -(으)시 is a honorific suffix used to show respect towards the subject of the sentence. It is added to verbs or adjectives

[1] ㄹ is omitted.
살으세요 (X)
선생님은 미국에서 사세요.
My teacher lives in the U.S.

❷ Rules

If the stem ends in a consonant → Stem + 으시	
읽다 (to read) → 읽 + 으시 + 다 → 읽으시다	
If the stem ends in a vowel or ㄹ → Stem + 시	
가다 (to go) → 가 + 시 + 다 → 가시다	
살다 (to live) → 사 + 시 + 다 → 사시다[1]	

[2] Originally, (으)셔요 was the standard form.
으시+어요→으시어요→으셔요
However, (으)세요 was also recognized as standard. Now, both are correct, but (으)세요 is more commonly used.

Formal Polite	V/A(으)십니다 [eu·sim·ni·da]	읽으십니다 / 가십니다
Informal Polite	V/A(으)세요 [eu·se·yo][2]	읽으세요 / 가세요
Casual	V/A(으)셔 [eu·syeo]	읽으셔 / 가셔

선생님이 신문을 읽으세요.   The teacher is reading the newspaper.
할머니가 병원에 가세요.   My grandmother is going to the hospital.

Irregular conjugation for verbs ending in ㄷ and ㅂ

듣다 → 들으시다 (들으세요)
돕다 → 도우시다 (도우세요)

❸ When to use -(으)시

▶ -(으)시 is used when the subject of the sentence is a person who is older, of higher status, or someone whom the speaker wishes to show respect.[3]

If you're talking with your grandmother about your friend:
제 친구는 구글에서 일해요. My friend works at Google.
→ Since the subject is '친구(friend)', '일해요' with (으)시 is not used.

If you're talking with your friend about your grandmother:
우리 할머니는 영어를 배우셔. My grandmother is learning English.
→ Since the subject is '할머니(grandmother)', '배우셔' with (으)시 is used.

[3] While the level of speech depends on the relationship between the speaker and the listener, the use of -(으)시 depends on the relationship between the speaker and the subject. Therefore, (으)시 is not always used in formal or polite speech.

Master Grammar By Practicing!

PRACTICE

🎧 04-01P.mp3

A Change the word into the honorific basic form, using '-(으)시'.

앉다	→	<u>앉으시다</u>	사다	→	<u>사시다</u>

1. 배우다 → _____ 2. 살다 → _____
3. 씻다 → _____ 4. 굽다 → _____
5. 받다 → _____ 6. 슬프다 → _____

B Change the given verb to complete the sentence using '-(으)세요'.

재미있다 (to be fun)	→	저희 할머니는 <u>재미있으세요.</u>

1.   끄다 (to turn off)   →   어머니가 불을 _____

2.   괜찮다 (to be okay)   →   할머니가 아팠어요. 하지만 지금은 _____

3.   바꾸다 (to change)   →   어머니가 백화점에서 옷을 _____

4.   사다 (to buy)   →   선생님이 시장에서 그릇을 _____

C Change the underlined word into '-(으)시다' form according to all levels of speech.

할아버지가 노래를 잘 <u>부르다</u>.	→	<u>부르십니다 / 부르세요 / 부르셔</u>

1.   아주머니가 가방에서 열쇠를 <u>꺼내다</u>.   →   _____ / _____ / _____

2.   아저씨가 뉴스를 <u>보다</u>.   →   _____ / _____ / _____

3.   선생님이 볼펜으로 편지를 <u>쓰다</u>.   →   _____ / _____ / _____

4.   할머니가 김치찌개를 <u>만들다</u>.   →   _____ / _____ / _____

WORDS

불 [bul] fire   끄다 [kkeu·da] to turn off   괜찮다 [gwaen·chan·ta] to be okay

시장 [si·jang] market   그릇 [geu·reut] bowl   열쇠 [yeol·soe] key

꺼내다 [kkeo·nae·da] to take out   뉴스 [nyu·seu] news   볼펜 [bol·pen] ballpoint pen

🎧 04-02G.mp3

사장님께서 음료수를 주셨어요.
The boss gave me a drink.

할머니께 전화할 거예요.
I will call my grandmother.

Honorific Particles

Some particles have separate honorific forms. These particles are generally used with people who are significantly older or in a higher social position, such as teachers, bosses, or elders.

❶ N이/가 → N께서 [kke·seo] : Subject Particle

▶ 께서 is a honorific version of '이/가', which are subject particles. It highlights the subject of a sentence in a respectful manner.

선생님께서 한국어를 가르치세요. The teacher teaches Korean.
할머니께서 저희 집에 오셨어요. My grandmother came to our house.

❷ N은/는 → N께서는 [kke·seo·neun] : Topic Particle

▶ 께서는 combines the subject marker '께서' with '는', a topic particle.

사장님께서는 배를 좋아하세요. The boss likes pears.
할머니께서는 비빔밥을 시키셨어요. My grandmother ordered bibimbap.

❸ N에게 (한테) → N께 [kke] : to

▶ 께 is used to indicate the recipient of an action towards someone you highly respect.

할아버지께 선물을 보낼 거예요. I will send a gift to my grandfather.
손님께 떡을 서비스로 주었어요.
We gave rice cakes as a free service to the customer.

WORDS

음료수 [eum·ryo·su] beverage   배 [bae] pear   떡 [tteok] rice cake
시키다 [si·ki·da] to order (food)   서비스 [sseo·bi·seu] service (provided free of charge)

Master Grammar By Practicing!

🎧 04-02P.mp3

A Change the word into the honorific form.

| 사장님이 | → | 사장님께서 | 선생님에게 | → | 선생님께 |

1. 어머니는 → _____
2. 손님에게 → _____
3. 할아버지가 → _____
4. 제니의 아버지에게 → _____

B Choose the correct option.

| My grandfather made Japchae. | → 할아버지(께 / 께서) 잡채를 만드셨어요. |

1. I sent an email to the teacher. → (선생님께 / 선생님께서) 이메일을 보냈어요.
2. The customer changed the menu. → (손님께 / 손님께서) 메뉴를 바꾸셨어요.
3. My uncle sometimes comes to our house. → (삼촌께서는 / 삼촌께) 가끔 저희 집에 오세요.
4. I will give a hat as a gift to my grandmother. → 모자를 (할머니께 / 할머니께서는) 선물할 거예요.

C Fill in the blank with the given word using '께서' or '께'.

| 삼촌 (uncle) | → | 삼촌께서 신문을 읽으세요. |

1. 다니엘의 이모 (Daniel's aunt) → _____ 다니엘 결혼식에 오셨어요.
2. 할아버지 (grandfather) → 우리 엄마가 _____ 자주 가셔.
3. 부모님 (parents) → _____ 저에게 매달 이십 만원을 주세요.
4. 사장님 (boss) → _____ 새 프로그램을 설명할 거예요.

WORDS

잡채 [jap·chae] glass noodle dish   메뉴 [me·nyu] menu   삼촌 [sam·chon] uncle
가끔 [ga·kkeum] sometimes   이모 [i·mo] aunt
프로그램 [peu·ro·geu·ram] program   설명하다 [seol·myeong·ha·da] to explain

UNIT 3 | Special Honorific Words

🎧 04-03G.mp3

어머니께서 일찍 주무세요? 교수님, 생신이 어떻게 되세요?
Does your mother go to bed early? Professor, when is your birthday?

Some verbs and nouns in Korean use different word forms to express respect towards others.

① Honorific Verbs: When showing respect to the subject

Basic Form	Honorific Form	-요 Ending
먹다 (to eat) / 마시다 (to drink)	드시다 [deu·si·da] / 잡수시다[1] [jap·su·si·da]	드세요 [deu·se·yo] / 잡수세요 [jap·su·se·yo]
자다 (to sleep)	주무시다 [ju·mu·si·da]	주무세요 [ju·mu·se·yo]
말하다(to speak)	말씀하시다[mal·sseum·ha·si·da]	말씀하세요 [mal·sseum·ha·se·yo]
있다 (to exist)	계시다 [gye·si·da]	계세요 [gye·se·yo]
죽나 (to die)	돌아가시다 [do·ra·ga·si·da]	돌아가셨어요[2] [do·ra·ga·ssyeot·sseo·yo]

할아버지께서 저녁을 드셨어요? Did grandfather have dinner?
어제 안녕히 주무셨어요? Did you sleep well yesterday?

② Honorific Verbs: When showing respect to the target

Basic Form	Honorific Form	-요 Ending
말하다(to speak)	말씀드리다 [mal·sseum·deu·ri·da]	말씀드려요 [mal·sseum·deu·ryeo·yo]
주다 (to give)	드리다 [deu·ri·da]	드려요 [deu·ryeo·yo]
묻다 (to ask)	여쭙다 [yeo·jjup·tta]	여쭤요 [yeo·jjwo·yo] (=여쭈어요)
보다/만나다 (to meet)	뵙다 [boep·tta]	봬요 [bwae·yo] (=뵈어요)

어제 아버지께 말씀드렸어요. I spoke to my father yesterday.
선생님께 선물을 드릴 거예요. I am going to give a gift to the teacher.
교수님,[3] 내일 뵐 수 있어요? Professor, can I see you tomorrow?

---

[1] 잡수시다 is a higher level of formality compared to 드시다. It is used in very formal settings. 드시다 is more commonly used.

[2] Since someone is already deceased, it is written in the past tense as 돌아가셨어요.

[3] 님 is used after professional titles or names. This suffix elevates the status of the person: 선생님 (teacher), 교수님 (professor), 부모님 (parents), 사장님 (boss)

WORDS 죽다 [juk·tta] to die 교수님 [gyo·su·nim] professor

❸ Honorific Nouns

Basic Form	Honorific Form	Basic Form	Honorific Form
말 (words, talk)	말씀 [mal·sseum]	나이 (age)	연세 [yeon·se]
생일 (birthday)	생신 [saeng·sin]	이름 (name)	성함 [seong·ham]
밥 (meal, food)	진지 [jin·ji]	사람 (person)	분 [bun]
집 (house)	댁 [daek]		

[4]어떻게 되세요? is a polite and indirect way of asking about someone's information. 성함이 어떻게 되세요? literally translates as "How does your name become?", but in English, it is translated as "What is your name?" or more respectfully, "May I ask what your name is?".

사장님, 성함이 어떻게 되세요?[4] Sir/Madam President, what is your name?

그분은 연세가 어떻게 되세요? How old is he/she(that person)?

Master Grammar By Practicing!

PRACTICE

🎧 04-03P.mp3

A Change the underlined verb to the honorific form.

작년에 영수의 할아버지가 <u>죽었어요.</u>	→	<u>돌아가셨어요.</u>

1. 할아버지, 어제 술 많이 <u>마셨어요?</u> → _____
2. 선생님께서 모두 운동장에 <u>있어요.</u> → _____
3. 어머니께 선물로 가방을 <u>줄 거예요.</u> → _____
4. 선생님, 요즘 잘 <u>자요?</u> → _____

B Correct the underlined part.

내일이 교수님 <u>생일이세요.</u>	→	내일이 교수님 <u>생신이세요.</u>

1. 사장님, <u>나이가</u> 어떻게 되세요? → 사장님, _____ 어떻게 되세요?
2. 부모님께 생신 선물을 <u>줬어요.</u> → 부모님께 생신 선물을 _____
3. 학교에 선생님께서 <u>몇 사람 있어요?</u> → 학교에 선생님께서 _____
4. <u>할아버지는 말이</u> 적으세요. → _____ 적으세요.

WORDS 운동장 [un·dong·jang] sports field   적다 [jeok·tta] to be litte, to be few

🎧 04-C.mp3

헨리: 유나 씨는 주말에 뭐했어요? What did you do on the weekend?

유나: 집에서 할머니랑 드라마 봤어요
I watched a drama at home with my grandmother.

헨리: 할머니께서 유나 씨랑 같이 사세요?
Does your grandmother live with you?

유나: 아니요, 할머니 댁은 부산이에요. No, her house is in Busan.

토요일에 서울에 오셨어요. She came to Seoul on Saturday.

헨리: 유나 씨는 할머니랑 친해요? Are you close with your grandmother?

유나: 네, 저는 할머니가 진짜 좋아요. Yes, I really love my grandmother.

헨리: 할머니께서는 부산에서 혼자 사세요? Does she live alone in Busan?

유나: 네, 혼자 계세요. 할아버지께서 작년에 돌아가셨어요.
Yes, she is alone. My grandfather passed away last year

그래서 할머니께 자주 전화해요. So I call her often.

✎ Using honorific particles or words is not always mandatory. Especially with my family members, with whom I have a close relationship, it's natural not to use such language. However, it is polite to use these forms when addressing the elder family members of others.

RECAP CHAPTER 4

❶ A/V-(으)시: Honorific Suffix

If the word stem ends in a consonant → stem + 으시
If the word stem ends in a vowel → stem + 시

	Statement	Question
Formal polite	A/V-으십니다 / A/V-십니다 읽으십니다 / 가십니다	A/V-으십니까? / A/V-십니까? 읽으십니까? / 가십니까?
Informal polite	A/V-으세요 / A/V-세요 읽으세요 / 가세요	A/V-으세요? / A/V-세요? 읽으세요? / 가세요?
Casual	A/V-으셔 / A/V-셔 읽으셔 / 가셔	A/V-으셔? / A/V-셔? 읽으셔? / 가셔?

❷ Honorific Particles

N께서: The honorific form of the subject particles 이/가.
N께서는: The honorific form of the topic particles 은/는.
N께: The honorific form of 에게(한테), indicating the recipient or direction of an action.

❸ Honorific Words

To the subject		To the target of the action		Noun	
먹다, 마시다	드시다	묻다	여쭙다	나이	연세
자다	주무시다	주다	드리다	생일	생신
말하다	말씀하시다	말하다	말씀드리다	말	말씀
있다	계시다	보다, 만나다	뵙다	이름	성함
죽다	돌아가시다			밥	진지
				사람	분
				집	댁

REVIEW TEST CHAPTER 4

A Choose the option where the honorific form is used correctly.

> 민호: 할아버지 집에 있다?
> Is your grandfather at home?
> 제니: 네, 그런데 지금 자다.
> Yes, but he's sleeping.

① 계세요 - 자세요 ② 계세요 - 주무세요
③ 있으세요 - 자세요 ④ 있어요 - 주무세요

B Choose the option with the **incorrectly** paired honorific forms.

① 생일 - 생신
② 나이 - 연세
③ 이름 - 성녕
④ 말 - 말씀

C Choose the **incorrect** sentence.

① 할머니께서 말씀하셨어요.
② 할머니께 말씀드렸어요.
③ 할머니께 선물을 주었어요.
④ 할머니께서 저에게 선물을 주셨어요.

D Choose the option where the particle is correctly changed to its honorific form.

① 선생님이 → 선생님께서는
② 부모님은 → 부모님께서
③ 교수님한테 → 교수님께서는
④ 아버지가 → 아버지께서

E Choose the correct option.

> He is my grandfather
> → _____은 제 할아버지 _____.

① 저분, 세요 ② 저 남자, 세요
③ 저 남자, 예요 ④ 저분, 예요

F In the following passage, choose the option that is written **incorrectly**.

> ①할아버지께서 미국에 ②살으세요. 저희 가족은 일년에 한 번 정도 미국에 가요. 미국에서 할아버지를 ③뵈요. 저희는 호텔에 가지 않아요. 할아버지 ④댁에서 지내요.

G Read the following dialogue and choose the **incorrect** statement.

> 민호: 교수님 계세요?
> 연주: 오늘 교수님 생신이세요.
> 그래서 학교에 안 오셨어요.
> 무슨 일이세요?
> 민호: 교수님께 이걸 드릴 거예요.
> 연주: 저한테 주세요.
> 제가 교수님께 말씀드릴게요.
> 성함이 어떻게 되세요?
> 민호: 제 이름은 이민호예요.

① 교수님은 오늘 생신입니다.
② 민호는 교수님를 못 만났습니다.
③ 연주가 교수님 댁에 갑니다.
④ 민호는 연주에게 이름을 말합니다.

🎧 04-V.mp3

No.	✓	Word	Meaning
1	☐	교수님	
2	☐	가끔	
3	☐	열쇠	
4	☐	프로그램	
5	☐	적다	
6	☐	메뉴	
7	☐	끄다	
8	☐	배 (fruit)	
9	☐	꺼내다	
10	☐	서비스	
11	☐	시장	
12	☐	시키다	
13	☐	죽다	
14	☐	음료수	
15	☐	볼펜	
16	☐	떡	
17	☐	잡채	
18	☐	이모	
19	☐	그릇	
20	☐	설명하다	
21	☐	삼촌	
22	☐	괜찮다	
23	☐	불	
24	☐	뉴스	
25	☐	운동장	

Number of words I've learned: _____ / 25

National Symbols of South Korea

National symbols are animal, flora, or other abstract representations - or some distinctive object - that over time have become closely associated with a country or entity. South Korea has not officially designated natural elements as national symbols apart from the flag or national anthem, but there are many unofficial symbols recognized by convention.

Korea's Flower, 무궁화 Mugunghwa (Rose of Sharon)

The Mugunghwa, long cherished by the Korean people, symbolizes the nation with its meaning of 'a flower that blooms forever and never dies'. Historical records show that even before ancient Korea, the Korean people considered mugunghwa as a precious flower from the heavens. Mugunghwa gained even more love from the people after the phrase "무궁화 삼천리 화려강산" was included in the national anthem.

Korea's Tree, 소나무 Sonamu (Pine Tree)

The pine tree is indispensable in the history of the Korean nation. The name pine(솔) signifies excellence, a quality that made it the exclusive choice for constructing royal palaces. Pine trees symbolize resilience and endurance, keeping their green appearance even in harsh winter weather. There may be similarities between the pine trees and the history of Korea, where they have survived and protected themselves through constant invasion and oppression.

Korea's Animal, 호랑이 Horangi (Tiger)

Tigers have appeared widely in Korean art and folklore, from the founding myths of Korea to many folktales, and are beloved by many Koreans. There is a Korean idiom "호랑이 담배 피던 시절 (the time when tigers smoked cigarettes)" which means the distant past. Tigers have traditionally served as a talisman to ward off evil in Korea, as bravery and strength of the tiger symbolize protection. In maps depicting the Korean Peninsula, a tiger is portrayed as a figure leaning toward the continent with its forelimbs, representing Korea facing the continent.

CHAPTER 5
Imperatives and Requests

UNIT 1 V-(으)세요 (do)

UNIT 2 V-지 마세요 (do not)

UNIT 3 V-아/어 주세요 (please do)

What you'll learn in this chapter

In Chapter 5, we focus on the crucial aspects of giving instructions and making requests in Korean. You'll learn the art of framing requests and instructions in a way that's considerate and culturally appropriate. From asking someone to do something for you to politely telling them not to do something, this chapter provides the tools you need to communicate effectively and respectfully in various social contexts.

UNIT 1   V-(으)세요 (do)

🎧 05-01G.mp3

25번 버스를 타세요.
Please take bus number 25.

이 의자에 앉으세요.
Please sit in this chair.

❶ V-(으)세요 [(eu)·se·yo] : **do**

▶ -(으)세요 form is a polite imperative, used to ask someone to do something or to give a suggestion or command in a polite manner.

❷ Rules[1]

If the stem ends in a consonant	→ Stem + 으세요
읽다 (to read) → 읽 + 으세요	→ 읽으세요
If the stem ends in a vowel or ㄹ	→ Stem + 세요
가다 (to do) → 가 + 세요	→ 가세요
만들다 (to make) → 만들 + 세요	→ 만드세요[2]

Formal Polite	V-(으)십시오 [eu·sip·si·o][2]	읽으십시오 / 가십시오
with -시-	V-(으)세요 [eu·se·yo][3]	읽으세요 / 가세요
Informal Polite	V-아/어요 [a/eo·yo]	읽어요 / 가요
Casual	V-아/어 [a/eo]	읽어 / 가

문을 닫으십시오. Please close the door.

책 20쪽을 읽으세요. Please read page 20 of the book.

정류장에서 버스를 기다려요. Wait for the bus at the bus stop.

이따가[4] 우리집으로 와. Come to my house later.

⚠ Imperative forms are typically used with verbs in the present tense, although there are idiomatic exceptions with adjectives such as '건강하다' (to be healthy) and '행복하다' (to be happy).[5]

[1] All forms other than the formal polite form are identical to declarative sentences.

[2] The (으)십시오 form conveys a sense of official or formal authority, making it used in public announcements and formal instructions.

[3] The (으)세요 form is the most commonly used in everyday conversation due to its polite yet friendly tone.

[4] 이따가 indicates a relatively near future, typically within a few hours or less.

[5] Examples:
할머니, 건강하세요!
Grandma, stay healthy!
올해에도 행복하세요! Be happy this year too!

WORDS

쪽 [jjok] page   정류장 [jeong·ryu·jang] bus stop   이따가 [i·tta·ga] later
건강하다 [geon·gang·ha·da] to be healthy   행복하다 [haeng·bok·ha·da] to be happy

Master Grammar By Practicing!

🎧 05-01P.mp3

A Change the underlined verb to the imperative form using '-(으)세요'.

오다 (to come)	→	오늘 저녁에 저희 집으로 <u>오세요.</u>

1. 나가다 (to go out) → 지금 밖으로 _____
2. 켜다 (to turn on) → 방마다 불을 _____
3. 쉬다 (to rest) → 오늘은 집에서 _____
4. 입다 (to wear) → 내일 검은색 옷을 _____

B Change the underlined verb into imperative form according to all levels of speech.

여기에 이름과 전화번호를 <u>쓰다</u>.	→	<u>쓰십시오 / 쓰세요 / 써요 / 써</u>

1. 생일 파티에 <u>오다</u>. → _____ / _____ / _____
2. 창문을 <u>닫다</u>. → _____ / _____ / _____
3. 저 정류장에서 버스를 <u>갈아타다</u>. → _____ / _____ / _____
4. 5쪽에서 10쪽까지 <u>읽다</u>. → _____ / _____ / _____

C Look at the pictures and write a corresponding imperative sentence using '-(으)세요'.

0. 문   1. 여권   2. 택시   3. 편지   4. 옷

열다 (to open) → <u>문을 여세요.</u>	

1. 가져오다 (to bring) → _____
2. 타다 (to take) → _____
3. 보내다 (to send) → _____
4. 바꾸다 (to change) → _____

🎧 05-02G.mp3

그 드라마 보지 마세요.
Please do not watch that drama.

가방 들지 마. 너무 무거워.
Don't carry the bag. It's too heavy.

❶ V-지 마세요 [ji ma·se·yo] : **do not**

▶ -지 마세요 is the negative form of the imperative form V-(으)세요

▶ It's used to request or persuade the listener not to do a particular action.

▶ The -세요 ending adds politeness to the prohibition, making it suitable for addressing elders, strangers, or people in a higher social position.

❷ Rules

> It's irrelevant whether the verb stem is a consonant or a vowel,
>
> → Stem + 지 마세요[1]
>
> 앉다 (to sit)   → 앉 + 지 마세요 → 앉지 마세요
>
> 가다 (to go)   → 가 + 지 마세요 → 가지 마세요

[1] 마세요 is a word derived from the verb 말다[mal·da], which originally means 'to not do something' or 'to cease an action'.

Formal Polite	V-지 마십시오 [ji ma·sip·si·o][2]	앉지 마십시오 / 가지 마십시오
with -시-	V-지 마세요 [ji ma·se·yo]	앉지 마세요 / 가지 마세요
Informal Polite	V-지 마요 [ji ma·yo]	앉지 마요 / 가지 마요
Casual	V-지 마 [ji ma]	앉지 마 / 가지 마

[2] The 지 마십시오 form is commonly used in public announcements and formal instructions.

엘리베이터를 타지 마세요.   Please do not take the elevator.

박물관에 들어가지 마십시오.   Please do not enter the museum.

게임 너무 오래 하지 마요.   Don't play games for too long.

이 수건 쓰지 마. 안 깨끗해.   Don't use this towel. It's not clean.

WORDS

들다 [deul·da] to lift, to carry
들어가다 [deu·reo·ga·da] to enter

엘리베이터 [el·li·be·i·teo] elevator
오래 [o·rae] long (time)

수건 [su·geon] towel

Master Grammar By Practicing!

🎧 05-02P.mp3

A Change the underlined verb into negative imperative form according to all levels of speech.

물을 빨리 <u>마시다</u>.	→	<u>마시지 마십시오 / 마시지 마세요 / 마시지 마요 / 마시지 마</u>

1. 주말에는 <u>운동하다</u>. → _____ / _____ / _____ /
2. 2층에 <u>올라오다</u>. → _____ / _____ / _____ /
3. 창문을 <u>닫다</u>. → _____ / _____ / _____ /
4. 그 남자랑 <u>사귀다</u>. → _____ / _____ / _____ /

B Change the imperative sentence into the negative form using '-지 마세요'.

부모님께 <u>거짓말하세요</u>.	→	부모님께 <u>거짓말하지 마세요</u>.

1. 친구랑 오래 <u>전화하세요</u>. → 친구랑 오래 _____
2. 눈을 <u>감으세요</u>. → 눈을 _____
3. 공원에 <u>들어가세요</u>. → 공원에 _____
4. 쓰레기를 <u>버리세요</u>. → 쓰레기를 _____

C Answer the question using '-지 마세요'.

A: 요즘 너무 바빠요. (일을 많이 하다)	B: 그럼 <u>일을 많이 하지 마세요</u>.

1. A: 요즘 목이 너무 아파요. (담배를 피우다)   B: 그럼 _____
2. A: 요즘 다리가 너무 아파요. (많이 걷다)   B: 그럼 _____
3. A: 요즘 발이 너무 아파요. (구두를 신다)   B: 그럼 _____
4. A: 요즘 돈이 너무 없어요. (쇼핑을 하다)   B: 그럼 _____

WORDS

빨리 [ppal·li] quickly   올라오다 [ol·la·o·da] to come up   거짓말하다 [geo·jit·mal·ha·da] to lie

사귀다 [sa·gwi·da] to date (someone)   눈 [nun] eye   감다 [gam·tta] to close (eyes)

쓰레기 [sseu·re·gi] trash   버리다 [beo·ri·da] to throw away   목 [mok] neck   다리 [da·ri] leg

UNIT 3 ｜ V-아/어 주세요 (please do)

05-03G.mp3

천천히 말해 주세요.
Please speak slowly.

창문을 열어 주세요.
Please open the window.

❶ V-아/어 주세요 [a/eo ju·se·yo] : **please do**

▶ -아/어 주세요 is used in polite requests or to ask someone to do something for you.

▶ It is formed by attaching -아/어 to the verb stem, followed by 주세요, which literally means 'please give'.

[1] Easy way: Add 주세요 to the conjugated form (from which 요 is removed in the present tense).

❷ Rules[1]

> If the last vowel of the stem is ㅏ or ㅗ → Stem + 아 주세요
>
> 오다 (to come) → 오 + 아 주세요 → 와 주세요
>
> If the last vowel of the stem is neither ㅏ nor ㅗ → Stem + 어 주세요
>
> 읽다 (to read) → 읽 + 어 주세요 → 읽어 주세요
>
> For all of the words ending with 하다 → 하 + 여 주세요 → 해주세요
>
> 말하다 (to speak) → 말하 + 여 주세요 → 말해 주세요

The principle is to write 아/어 and 주세요 separately, but writing them together is also allowed.

Formal Polite	V-아/어 주십시오 [a/eo ju·sip·si·o]	와 주십시오 / 읽어 주십시오
with -시-	V-아/어 주세요 [a/eo ju·se·yo]	와 주세요 / 읽어 주세요
Informal Polite	V-아/어 줘요 [a/eo jwo·yo]	와 줘요 / 읽어 줘요
Casual	V-아/어 줘 [a/eo jwo]	와 줘 / 읽어 줘

김밥 좀[2] 만들어 주세요.   Please make some gimbap.

내일 이사 좀 도와 주세요.   Please help me move tomorrow.

전화번호를 알려 주십시오.   Please let me know your phone number.

이 단어 좀 찾아 줘.   Please look up this word.

[2] 좀 is an abbreviation for 조금 (a little), and it is also used to soften the tone when making a request. It is often used with the -아/어 주세요 pattern.

WORDS

천천히 [cheon·cheon·hi] slowly	**이사** [i·sa] move (residence)	**알리다** [al·li·da] to inform
단어 [da·neo] word	**찾다** [chat·tta] to find	

Master Grammar By Practicing!

🎧 05-03P.mp3

A Change the given verb to complete the sentence using '-아/어 주세요'.

대답하다 (to answer)	→	제 질문에 대답해 주세요.

1. 운전하다 (to drive) → 천천히 _____
2. 오다 (to come) → 제 생일 파티에 _____
3. 고르다 (to choose) → 선물 좀 _____ .
4. 끄다 (to turn off) → 불 좀 _____

B Change the underlined verb into '-아/어 주다' form according to all levels of speech.

얼굴을 그리다.	→	그려 주십시오 / 그려 주세요 / 그려 줘요 / 그려 줘

1. 택시를 부르다. → _____ / _____ / _____ / _____
2. 이 의자에 앉다. → _____ / _____ / _____ / _____
3. 잠시 기다리다. → _____ / _____ / _____ / _____
4. 사과를 씻다. → _____ / _____ / _____ / _____

C Choose the corresponding verb and change it into '-아/어 주세요' form.

보이다   바꾸다   사다   돕다   찾다

배가 너무 아파요. 약국에서 약 좀 사 주세요.

1. 숙제가 너무 많아요. 숙제 좀 _____
2. 학생이에요? 그럼 학생증을 _____
3. 제 콘서트 표가 없어요! 표 좀 _____
4. 신발이 너무 커요. 이 신발 좀 _____

WORDS

질문 [jil·mun] question
잠시 [jam·si] for a moment
콘서트 [kon·seo·teu] concert

대답하다 [dae·dap·ha·da] to answer
학생증 [hak·saeng·jeung] student ID
표 [pyo] ticket

얼굴 [eol·gul] face
보이다 [bo·i·da] to show

🎧 05-C.mp3

마리아: 지수 씨, 저 좀 도와 주세요. Jisoo, please help me.

이 한국어 단어를 모르겠어요. I don't understand this Korean word.

지수: 무슨 단어예요? What word is it?

마리아: 이 단어 좀 보세요. 이거 언제 쓸 수 있어요?
Please look at this word. When can I use it?

지수: 이 말은 쓰지 마세요. Please don't use this word.

사람들이 기분 나쁠 거예요. People would feel bad.

마리아: 정말요? 그런데 유튜브에서 썼어요. Really? But It's used on YouTube.

지수: 친구한테는 괜찮을 수 있어요. It could be okay with friends.

마리아: 아, 한국말은 너무 어려워요. Ah, Korean is so difficult.

지수 씨가 저 좀 가르쳐 주세요. Please teach me.

지수: 그래요. 그럼 매주 토요일에 도서관으로 오세요.
Sure. Then come to the library every Saturday.

✏️ 모르겠어요 [mo·reu·get·sseo·yo] is used when you don't understand something or are unsure. It is a more polite form than 몰라요 and implies thoughtful consideration or uncertainty.

✏️ 기분 좋다 [gi·bun jo·ta]: to feel good, to be pleased, 기분 나쁘다 [gi·bun na·ppeu·da]: to feel bad, to be upset

RECAP CHAPTER 5

❶ V-(으)세요, V-지 마세요: Imperative Sentences

Positive Form (Informal Polite with -시-):
If the verb stem ends in a consonant → stem + 으세요
If the verb stem ends in a vowel → stem + 세요

Negative Form (Informal Polite with -시-):
stem + 지 마세요

	Positive	Negative
Formal polite	V-으십시오 / V-십시오 앉으십시오 / 가십시오	V-지 마십시오 앉지 마십시오 / 가지 마십시오
Informal Polite with -시-	V-으세요 / V-세요 앉으세요 / 가세요	V-지 마세요 앉지 마세요 / 가지 마세요
Informal Polite	V-아요 / V-어요 / V-해요 앉아요, 가요 / 먹어요 / 일해요	V-지 마요 앉지 마요 / 가지 마요
Casual	V-아 / V-어 / V-해 앉아, 가 / 먹어 / 일해	V-지 마 앉지 마 / 가지 마

❷ V-아/어 주세요: Request Sentences

If the last vowel of the verb stem is ㅏ or ㅗ → stem + 아 주세요
If the last vowel of the verb stem is neither ㅏ nor ㅗ → stem + 어 주세요
Every verb with 하다 → 하다 changes to 해 주세요

Formal polite	V-아/어 주십시오	와 주십시오 / 읽어 주십시오 / 말해 주십시오
Informal Polite with -시-	V-아/어 주세요	와 주세요 / 읽어 주세요 / 말해 주세요
Informal Polite	V-아/어 줘요	와 줘요 / 읽어 줘요 / 말해 줘요
Casual	V-아/어 줘	와 줘 / 읽어 줘 / 말해 줘

REVIEW TEST CHAPTER 5

A Choose the option that is paired with the correct answers.

> 교실에서 (   ).
> Please leave the classroom.
>
> 음악을 (   ).
> Please listen to the music.

① 나가십시오 - 듣으십시오
② 나가으십시오 - 듣으십시오
③ 나가십시오 - 들으십시오
④ 나가으십시오 - 들으십시오

B Choose the correct sentence.

① 10시까지 기다리세요.
② 부모님을 도우세요.
③ 저에게 한국어를 배워세요.
④ 창문을 열으세요.

C Choose the incorrect sentence.

① 이 음식을 드시지 마세요.
② 그 나라에서 살지 마세요.
③ 고기를 구지 마세요.
④ 저 방에 들어가지 마세요.

D Choose the dialogue that does not make sense.

① A: 배가 고파.   B: 밥을 먹어.
② A: 머리가 아파.   B: 집에서 쉬어.
③ A: 심심해.   B: 영화를 봐.
④ A: 배가 아파.   B: 담배를 피워.

E Choose the correct form of the underlined verb in the '-아/어 주세요' form.

> 전화번호를 알리다.
> 제 숙제를 돕다.

① 알려 주세요 - 돕아 주세요
② 알려 주세요 - 도와 주세요
③ 알랴 주세요 - 도와 주세요
④ 알랴 주세요 - 돕아 주세요

F Read the following dialogue and choose the incorrect statement.

> 제니: 저 요즘 잠을 잘 못 자요.
> 다니엘: 저처럼 매일 아침 운동해요.
>   그럼 더 잘 잘 거예요.
> 제니: 운동이요? 전 일찍 못 일어나요.
> 다니엘: 할 수 있어요.
>   내일 아침부터 저랑 같이 운동해요!
> 제니: 네, 그래요.
>   그럼 아침 일곱 시에 전화해 주세요.
> 다니엘: 전화 받으세요!

① 제니는 잠을 잘 못 잡니다.
② 다니엘은 매일 아침 운동을 합니다.
③ 제니는 다니엘과 함께 운동할 것입니다.
④ 제니가 다니엘에게 전화할 것입니다.

🎧 05-V.mp3

No.	✓	Word	Meaning	No.	✓	Word	Meaning
1	☐	들다		26	☐	감다	
2	☐	전화번호		27	☐	이사	
3	☐	잠시		28	☐	빨리	
4	☐	찾다		29	☐	건강하다	
5	☐	엘리베이터		30	☐	쪽	
6	☐	이따가		31	☐	질문	
7	☐	거짓말하다		32	☐	행복하다	
8	☐	버리다		33	☐	수건	
9	☐	쓰레기		34	☐	표	
10	☐	얼굴		35	☐	사귀다	
11	☐	보이다		36	☐	검은색	
12	☐	목		37	☐	택시	
13	☐	정류장		38	☐	들어가다	
14	☐	나가다		39	☐	눈	
15	☐	단어		40	☐	천천히	
16	☐	알리다		41	☐	학생증	
17	☐	대답하다					
18	☐	올라오다					
19	☐	콘서트					
20	☐	켜다					
21	☐	여권					
22	☐	갈아타다					
23	☐	오래					
24	☐	다리					
25	☐	번호					

Number of words I've learned: _____ / 41

A Guide to Iconic Korean Street Foods

Street foods in Korea captivate the taste buds of the people with their diverse varieties and flavors. Particularly, the following street foods are beloved as representative desserts and snacks in Korea.

붕어빵 Bungeoppang

Bungeoppang is characterized by its cute fish-shaped appearance, baked in a special metal mold. Traditionally filled with sweet red bean paste, it can also contain various other fillings like cream, cheese, or even chocolate. Bungeoppang is favored as a light snack for its portability and is especially popular on cold days.

호떡 Hotteok

Hotteok, a traditional Korean dessert, is a popular street food easily found at street vendors or traditional markets. It consists of dough with sweet filling, cooked until soft and crispy. The dough is filled with sweet red bean paste and then cooked, making Hotteok loved by many for its sweet flavor and soft texture. It evokes childhood memories and warm feelings among Koreans.

닭꼬치 Dak-kkochi (Chicken Skewers)

Dak-kkochi is commonly sold on the streets, appreciated for their convenience as they are easy to hold and eat. Typically, they are prepared by cutting chicken into small pieces, skewering them on sticks, and then grilling them with various seasonings, sometimes over charcoal.

핫도그 Hot Dog

Hot Dogs, beloved by many especially children and teenagers, are similar to corn dogs rather than traditional American hot dogs. Sausages are typically encased in bread dough and deep-fried. Hot dog shops offer various versions, including those filled with cheese or topped with potato fries.

CHAPTER 6
Hope and Will

What you'll learn in this chapter

In this chapter, we'll explore the various ways to express desires, wishes, and intentions in Korean. This chapter is all about conveying what you want to do, hope to happen, or plan to undertake. We will also discuss when and how to appropriately use these expressions, providing you with a comprehensive understanding of how to communicate your wishes and plans.

UNIT 1 | V-고 싶다 (I want)

🎧 06-01G.mp3

저희는 서울을 구경하고 싶어요.   저 아이가 귤을 먹고 싶어했어.
We want to sightsee in Seoul.   That child wanted to eat mandarins.

❶ V-고 싶다 [go sip·tta] : **to want**

▶ -고 싶다 is used to express a desire or a wish to do something.

▶ It can only be used, when the subject is either the first (I/we) or the second person (you).

❷ Rules

> It's irrelevant whether the verb stem is a consonant or a vowel,
> → Stem + 고 싶다
>
> 먹다 (to eat)   → 먹 + 고 싶다   → 먹고 싶다
> 가다 (to go)   → 가 + 고 싶다   ▸ 가고 싶다[2]

저는 오늘 저녁에 김치찌개를 먹고 싶어요.   I want to eat kimchi stew this evening.
내년에 한국에 가고 싶어요.   I want to go to Korea next year.

❸ V-고 싶어하다 [go si·peo·ha·da] : **to want (for the third person)**

▶ -고 싶어하다 is used to express that a third person (he, she, they) wants or desires to do something.[1]

> Stem + 고 싶어하다
> 먹다 (to eat)   → 먹 + 고 싶어하다   → 먹고 싶어하다
> 가다 (to go)   → 가 + 고 싶어하다   → 가고 싶어하다

제니는 포도를 먹고 싶어해요.   Jenny wants to eat grapes.
제니는 포도를 먹고 싶어요. (X)

✅ **Past tense of V고 싶다**
→ V-고 싶었다

저는 작년에 태국에 가고 싶었어요. I wanted to go to Thailand last year.

수지 씨, 초콜릿 먹고 싶었어요? Suzy, did you want to eat chocolate?

✅ When using the -고 싶다 pattern, 이/가 can be used to indicate the target of desire instead of 을/를, which marks the direct object.

저는 민호를 보고 싶어요. (O)
= 저는 민호가 보고 싶어요. (O)
I want to see Minho.
(I miss Minho.)

[1] 고 싶어하다 literally means 'seems to want to V'. It allows you to speak about others' desires in an indirect way.

WORDS   **구경하다** [gu·gyeong·ha·da] to sightsee, to look around   **귤** [gyul] mandarin orange
태국 [tae·guk] Thailand   **초콜릿** [cho·kol·lit] chocolate   **포도** [po·do] grape

Master Grammar By Practicing!

🎧 06-01P.mp3

A Change the given verb to complete the sentence using '-고 싶어요'.

| 읽다 (to read) | → | 저는 일본어 책을 <u>읽고 싶어요.</u> |

1. 쉬다 (to rest) → 저는 내일 집에서 _____
2. 사귀다 (to date) → 그 남자랑 _____
3. 살다 (to live) → 저랑 남편은 한국에서 _____
4. 운동하다 (to exercise) → 저는 매일 _____

B Choose the correct option between '-고 싶다' and '-고 싶어하다'.

| 언니는 파란색 신발을 (사고 싶어요 / 사고 싶어해요). |

1. 제니는 친구들을 파티에 (초대하고 싶어해요 / 초대하고 싶어요).
2. 저는 빨리 집에서 (씻고 싶어요 / 씻고 싶어해요).
3. 여러분, 제 음악 (듣고 싶어해요? / 듣고 싶어요?)
4. 헨리는 집에 (돌아가고 싶어했어요 / 돌아가고 싶었어요).

C Answer the question using '-고 싶다' or '-고 싶어하다', machting the tense of the question.

| A: 어제 뭐 하고 싶었어요? (구두를 사다) | B: 저는 <u>구두를 사고 싶었어요.</u> |

1. A: 내일 뭐 하고 싶어요? (친구랑 이야기하다)   B: 저는 내일 _____
2. A: 제니는 뭐 하고 싶어해요? (딸기를 먹다)   B: 제니는 _____
3. A: 동생은 뭐 하고 싶어했어요? (침대에 눕다)   B: 동생은 _____
4. A: 저녁에 뭐 하고 싶어요? (케이크를 만들다)   B: 저녁에 _____

WORDS

여러분 [yeo·reo·bun] (all of) you, everybody
이야기하다 [i·ya·gi·ha·da] to talk, to tell a story
눕다 [nup·tta] to lie down

돌아가다 [do·ra·ga·da] to return, to go back
딸기 [ddal·gi] strawberry

UNIT 2 | A/V-았/었으면 좋겠다 (I wish)

🎧 06-02G.mp3

돈이 많았으면 좋겠어요.
I wish I had a lot of money.

몸이 더 날씬했으면 좋겠어요.
I wish I were slimmer.

❶ A/V-았/었으면 좋겠다 [at/eot·sseu·myeon jo·ket·tta] : I wish

▶ -았/었으면 좋겠다 is used to express a wish or hope about a future event or a situation that has not yet occurred.

✅ -았/었으면 좋겠다 literally means 'I would like it if it had happened'.

❷ Rules

> If the last vowel of the stem is ㅏ or ㅗ → Stem + 았으면 좋겠어요
> 오다 (to come) → 오 + 았으면 좋겠어요 → 왔으면 좋겠어요
>
> If the last vowel of the stem is neither ㅏ nor ㅗ → Stem + 었으면 좋겠어요
> 쉬다 (to rest) → 쉬 + 었으면 좋겠어요 → 쉬었으면 좋겠어요
>
> For all of the words ending with 하다 → 했으면 좋겠어요
> 깨끗하다 (to be clean) → 깨끗했으면 좋겠어요

방학이 빨리 왔으면 좋겠어요. I wish the vacation would come soon.
더 오래 쉬었으면 좋겠어요. I wish I could rest for a longer time.
방이 깨끗했으면 좋겠어요. I wish the room were clean.

[1] Rules of A/V-(으)면 좋겠어요
If the stem ends in a consonant
→ stem + 으면 좋겠어요
먹다 → 먹으면 좋겠어요
If the stem ends in a vowel,
→ stem + 면 좋겠어요
보다 → 보면 좋겠어요

❸ A/V-(으)면 좋겠다[1] [(eu)·myeon jo·ket·tta] : I wish

▶ -(으)면 좋겠다 can be also used to express a wish or desire regarding a future.[2]

한국을 여행하면 좋겠어요. I wish to travel to Korea.
한국을 여행했으면 좋겠어요. I wish I had traveled to Korea.

[2] However, -았/었으면 좋겠다 conveys a stronger sense of longing or wish, as it presupposes the realization of a state that has not yet been achieved.

WORDS 몸 [mom] body   날씬하다 [nal·ssin·ha·da] to be slim

Master Grammar By Practicing!

🎧 06-02P.mp3

A Choose the correct option.

> 시험을 안 (봤으면 좋겠어요 / 보었으면 좋겠어요).

1. 날씨가 (좋었으면 좋겠어요 / 좋았으면 좋겠어요).

2. 더 일찍 (일어났으면 좋겠어요 / 일어나었으면 좋겠어요).

3. 집에 혼자 (있었으면 좋겠어요 / 있았으면 좋겠어요).

4. 회사가 더 (가깝웠으면 좋겠어요 / 가까웠으면 좋겠어요)

B Change the underlined verb to both '-(으)면 좋겠어요' and '-았/었으면 좋겠어요'.

> 아파트에 살다. → 아파트에 살면 좋겠어요 / 살았으면 좋겠어요.

1. 비가 오다. → 비가 _____ / _____

2. 콘서트 표가 싸다. → 콘서트 표가 _____ / _____

3. 시간이 많다. → 시간이 _____ / _____

4. 책을 더 읽다. → 책을 더 _____ / _____

C Make a sentence using the given words, as shown in the example.

> 저는 키가 작아요. (키, 크다) → 키가 컸으면 좋겠어요.

1. 여자친구가 떠났어요. (여자친구, 돌아오다) → _____

2. 요즘 너무 늦게 자요. (일찍, 자다) → _____

3. 저는 몸이 너무 약해요. (강하다) → _____

4. 한국어를 못해요. (한국어, 잘하다) → _____

WORDS

혼자 [hon·ja] alone   가깝다 [ga·kkap·tta] to be close   아파트 [a·pa·teu] apartment

비 [bi] rain   떠나다 [tteo·na·da] to leave   약하다 [yak·ha·da] to be weak

강하다 [gang·ha·da] to be strong   못하다 [mot·ha·da] to be bad (at)

🎧 06-03G.mp3

같이 영화 볼래요?
Do you want to watch a movie together?

저는 불고기 먹을래요.
I'd like to eat bulgogi.

❶ V-(으)ㄹ래요 [(eu)l·lae·yo]: I want

▶ -(으)ㄹ래요 is a verb ending used to express one's intention or will to do something in the future.

▶ This ending is polite yet casual, used in conversations among intimates such as friends, family, and acquaintances.

▶ -(으)ㄹ래요 is typically used in spoken language, can only be used with verbs[1], and is limited to the first-person subject (I).

[1] With adjectives, use -았/었으면 좋겠어요 instead.
저는 더 똑똑할래요. (X)
I will be smarter.
저는 더 똑똑했으면 좋겠어요. (O)
I wish I were smarter.

❷ Rules

If the stem ends in a consonant	→ Stem + 을래요
읽다 (to read) → 읽 + 을래요	→ 읽을래요
If the stem ends in a vowel or ㄹ	→ Stem + ㄹ래요
가다 (to go) → 가 + ㄹ래요	→ 갈래요
만들다 (to make) → 만들 + ㄹ래요	→ 만들래요

도서관에서 책 읽을래요.   I will read a book in the library.
공원에 갈래요.   I want to go to the park.

✓ In casual speech, remove 요 from -(으)ㄹ래요.
나는 콜라 마실래.
I want to drink cola.
영화 볼래?
Want to watch a movie?

❸ V-(으)ㄹ래요? [(eu)l·lae·yo]: Do you want to?/How about?

▶ -(으)ㄹ래요? is used to make polite offers or suggestions, or to ask about someone's intention or preference in a friendly, informal way.

내일 같이 점심 먹을래요?   Do you want to have lunch together tomorrow?
회의 준비 같이 하실래요?[2]   Would you like to prepare for the meeting together?

[2] When the relationship with the listener is close but the speaker still wants to show respect, -(으)실래요? (with -시- suffix) can be used.

WORDS   준비하다 [jun·bi·ha·da] to prepare

Master Grammar By Practicing!

A Change the underlined verb to the '-(으)ㄹ래요' form.

06-03P.mp3

> 저는 콜라 마시다.   →   저는 콜라 마실래요.

1. 저는 기숙사에서 살다. →   저는 기숙사에서 ＿＿＿＿＿＿
2. 저는 케이크 반만 먹다. →   저는 케이크 반만 ＿＿＿＿＿＿
3. 저는 이 바지 사다. →   저는 이 바지 ＿＿＿＿＿＿
4. 저는 커피에 설탕 넣다. →   저는 커피에 설탕 ＿＿＿＿＿＿

B Complete the answer using '-(으)ㄹ래요' or '-(으)ㄹ래', considering the level of formality.

> A: 집에 어떻게 갈 거예요? (택시, 타다)   B: 저는 택시 탈래요.

1. A: 점심 안 드세요? (이따가, 먹다)   B: 네, 배가 안 고파요. 저는 ＿＿＿＿＿＿＿＿
2. A: 차나 커피 마실래? (차, 마시다)   B: 응, 나는 ＿＿＿＿＿＿＿＿
3. A: 주말에 같이 등산할래요? (집, 쉬다)   B: 죄송해요. 저는 그냥 ＿＿＿＿＿＿＿＿
4. A: 무슨 옷 살래? (흰색 티셔츠, 사다)   B: 나는 ＿＿＿＿＿＿＿＿

C Choose the appropriate word and complete the the question, using '-(으)ㄹ래요?'.

| 올라가다 | 걷다 | 식사하다 | 만들다 | 배우다 |

> A: 주말에 저희 집에서 같이 식사할래요?   B: 네, 좋아요. 초대 감사합니다.

1. A: 회사까지 ＿＿＿＿＿＿＿   B: 아니요. 저는 다리가 아파요.
2. A: 우리랑 한국어 같이 ＿＿＿＿＿＿＿   B: 아니요, 저는 혼자 공부하고 싶어요.
3. A: 내일 지수 씨가 김밥 ＿＿＿＿＿＿＿   B: 죄송해요. 저는 김밥 만들 줄 몰라요.
4. A: 남산에 같이 ＿＿＿＿＿＿＿   B: 네, 좋아요! 저도 가고 싶었어요.

WORDS

기숙사 [gi·suk·sa] dormitory   **반** [ban] half   **설탕** [seol·tang] sugar
등산하다 [deung·san·ha·da] to hike   **차** [cha] tea   **흰색** [huin·saek] white
티셔츠 [ti·syeo·cheu] t-shirt

UNIT 4 | V-(으)ㄹ게요 (I will)

🎧 06-04G.mp3

시청에 다녀올게요.
I will go to the city hall and come back.

제가 소포를 받을게요.
I will receive the parcel.

❶ V-(으)ㄹ게요 [(eu)l·ge·yo] : **I will**

▶ -(으)ㄹ게요 is used when the speaker decides to do something or promises to do something in the future.

▶ This ending is polite yet casual, used in conversations among intimates such as friends, family, and acquaintances.

▶ It is typically used in spoken language.

▶ -(으)ㄹ게요 can only be used with verbs[1], and is limited to the first-person subject (I)[2], and cannot be used in questions[3].

❷ Rules

If the stem ends in a consonant	→ Stem + 을게요
읽다 (to read) → 읽 + 을게요	→ 읽을게요
If the stem ends in a vowel or ㄹ	→ Stem + ㄹ게요
가다 (to go) → 가 + ㄹ게요	→ 갈게요
만들다 (to make) → 만들 + ㄹ게요	→ 만들게요

이번 달에 책 다섯 권 읽을게요.   I will read five books this month.

내일 학교에 아홉 시까지 갈게요.   I will go to school by nine o'clock tomorrow.

❸ Difference between -(으)ㄹ게요 and -(으)ㄹ 거예요

▶ (으)ㄹ게요: Used to express intentions or thoughts with consideration for the listener.[4]

▶ (으)ㄹ 거예요: Used when the speaker is explaining personal decisions or plans.[4]

---

[1] With adjectives, use -(으)ㄹ 거예요 instead.
저는 키가 클게요. (X)
저는 키가 클 거예요. (O)
I will be tall.

[2] Use -(으)ㄹ 거예요 instead.
<u>엄마가</u> 내일 쇼핑할게요. (X)
<u>엄마가</u> 내일 쇼핑할 거예요. (O)
My mom will go shopping tomorrow.

[3] Use -(으)ㄹ 거예요 instead.
회의에 올게요? (X)
회의에 올 거예요? (O)
Will you come to the meeting?

[4] 병원에 갈게요.
I will go to the hospital.
(following advice from the other person)
병원에 갈 거예요.
I will go to the hospital.
(expressing a pre-decided matter)

WORDS

시청 [si·cheong] city hall   다녀오다 [da·nyeo·o·da] to go and come back
소포 [so·po] parcel

Master Grammar By Practicing!

A Change the verb to complete the sentence using '-(으)ㄹ게요'.

🎧 06-04P.mp3

쓰다 (to write)	→	이메일을 <u>쓸게요</u>.

1. 도와드리다 (to help) → 제가 꼭 _____

2. 오다 (to come) → 내일 일찍 _____

3. 열다 (to open) → 제가 문을 _____

4. 먹다 (to eat) → 밥을 조금만 _____

B Choose the correct option.

내일 아침에 바람이 많이 (불게요 / 불 거예요).

1. 바나나를 (가져올게요? / 가져올 거예요?)

2. 가방이 (비쌀게요 / 비쌀 거예요).

3. 민호가 곧 (올 거예요 / 올게요).

4. 저 지금 (내려갈게요? / 내려갈게요).

C Complete the answer using '-(으)ㄹ게요' or '-(으)ㄹ게', considering the level of formality.

A: 한국어 좀 가르쳐 줄 수 있어요? (가르쳐 주다)   B: 네, 제가 <u>가르쳐 줄게요</u>.

1. A: 나 이 반지 너무 가지고 싶어. (사 주다)   B: 그럼 내가 _____

2. A: 너무 추워요. 문 좀 닫아주세요. (닫다)   B: 제가 _____

3. A: 민호 씨, 오늘 너무 늦었어요. (오다)   B: 죄송해요. 내일은 일찍 _____

4. A: 이 핸드폰 어떻게 켜? (물어보다)   B: 내가 _____

WORDS

꼭 [kkok] certainly   바람 [ba·ram] wind   불다 [bul·da] to blow
내려가다 [nae·ryeo·ga·da] to go down   반지 [ban·ji] ring
가지다 [ga·ji·da] to have, to possess   물어보다 [mu·reo·bo·da] to ask

UNIT 5 | V-겠다 ① (I will)

06-05G.mp3

회의를 시작하겠습니다.
I will start the meeting.

학교 다녀오겠습니다.
I'm off to school.

① V-겠다 [get·tta] : I will, I plan to

▶ -겠다 is used to express the speaker's strong intention, decision or plan regarding the future.[1]

▶ It can only be used with the first-person subject (I) and only with verbs.

② Rules

Stem + 겠다	
먹다 (to eat) → 먹겠다	가다 (to go) → 가겠다

Formal Polite	V-겠습니다 [got·sseum ni·da][2]	먹겠습니다 / 가셌습니다
Informal Polite	V-겠어요 [get·sseo·yo]	먹겠어요 / 가겠어요
Casual	V-겠어 [get·sseo]	먹겠어 / 가겠어

제가 회의 장소로 가겠습니다.   I will go to the meeting place.
음식을 빨리 먹지 않겠어요.   I will not eat food quickly.

③ Idiomatic expressions using –겠

▶ 겠 is often idiomatically used in various Korean greetings, so make sure to remember the following useful expressions.

감사하겠습니다. I would be grateful.   잘 먹겠습니다.[3] Thank you for the meal.
다녀오겠습니다.[4] I will go and come back.
잘 부탁드리겠습니다.[5] I'm looking forward to being here.
처음 뵙겠습니다.[6] Nice to meet you.

[1] -겠다 is also used for making guesses. In that case, it can be used with both verbs and adjectives, and it can be used with all subjects. We will learn about this usage in Level 3.

[2] -겠다 is more commonly used in the formal polite form 겠습니다, particularly in settings such as formal speeches or announcements.

[3] 잘 먹겠습니다 literally means "I will eat well."

[4] 다녀오겠습니다 is used when leaving a place.

[5] 잘 부탁드리겠습니다 is used when seeking support or good relations.

[6] 처음 뵙겠습니다 is formal way to greet someone you're meeting for the first time.

WORDS

시작하다 [si·jak·ha·da] to start
처음 [cheo·eum] first

장소 [jang·so] place
부탁하다 [bu·tak·ha·da] to ask for a favor

Master Grammar By Practicing!

PRACTICE

🎧 06-05P.mp3

A Change the verb to complete the sentence, using '-겠습니다'.

| 시작하다 (to start) | → | 한국어 수업을 <u>시작하겠습니다</u>. |

1. 끝내다 (to finish) → 이번 주 금요일까지 그 일을 _____
2. 피우지 않다 (to not smoke) → 담배를 _____
3. 데려오다 (to bring peron) → 제가 그 학생을 _____
4. 말씀드리다 (to tell) → 지금 새 계획을 _____

B Change the given verb to complete the sentence, using '-겠어요'.

| 다이어트하다 (to do diet) | → | 내일부터 <u>다이어트를 하겠어요</u>. |

1. 공부하다 (to study) → 올해에는 한국어를 열심히 _____
2. 약속을 지키다 (to keep a promise) → 저는 _____
3. 마시지 않다 (to not drink) → 술을 _____
4. 일어나다 (to get up) → 내일부터 일찍 _____

C Match the Korean expressions with English translations.

1. I would be grateful.   a. 잘 부탁드리겠습니다.
2. Nice to meet you.   b. 잘 먹겠습니다.
3. I'm looking forward to being here.   c. 감사하겠습니다.
4. Thank you for the meal.   d. 학교 다녀오겠습니다.
5. I'm off to school.   e. 처음 뵙겠습니다.

WORDS

끝내다 [kkeut·nae·da] to finish   데려오다 [de·ryeo·o·da] to bring someone
계획 [gye·hoek] plan   다이어트 [da·i·eo·teu] diet
약속 [yak·sok] promise   지키다 [ji·ki·da] to keep (a promise)

🎧 06-C.mp3

요코: 민호 씨는 이번 방학에 뭐 할 거예요?
What are you going to do during this vacation?

민호: 이번 여름에 미국 여행을 하고 싶어요. I want to travel to the U.S. this summer.

그래서 영어를 잘 했으면 좋겠어요. So, I wish I were good at English.

요코: 저도요. 이번 방학에는 영어 공부를 열심히 할 거예요.
Me too. I will study English hard this vacation.

그래서 스터디 모임을 만들고 싶어요. So, I'd like to make a study group.

민호 씨도 같이 할래요? Would you like to join?

민호: 오, 좋아요! 저도 같이 할게요. Oh, I'd love to! I'll join too.

언제부터 시작해요? When are we starting?

요코: 다음 주부터 할 거예요. 제가 연락할게요. We'll start next week. I'll contact you.

민호: 네, 고마워요. 연락해요! Yes, thank you. Please contact me!

✏️ 모임 refers to a group of people coming together for a specific purpose, such as a social event, a study group, a business meeting, or any informal or formal assembly.

WORDS   모임 [mo·im] gathering, meeting   연락하다 [yeon·rak·ha·da] to contact

RECAP CHAPTER 6

❶ V-고 싶다: I want

	Statement	Question
Formal polite	V-고 싶습니다	V-고 싶습니까?
Informal polite	V-고 싶어요	V-고 싶어요?
Casual	V-고 싶어	V-고 싶어?

❷ A/V-았/었으면 좋겠다: I wish

	Statement	Question
Formal polite	A/V-았/었으면 좋겠습니다	A/V-았/었으면 좋겠습니까?
Informal polite	A/V-았/었으면 좋겠어요	A/V-았/었으면 좋겠어요?
Casual	A/V-았/었으면 좋겠어	A/V-았/었으면 좋겠어?

❸ V-(으)ㄹ래요: I want (in spoken language)

	Statement (I want-)	Question (Do you want-?)
Informal polite	V-(으)ㄹ래요	V-(으)ㄹ래요?
Casual	V-(으)ㄹ래	V-(으)ㄹ래?

❹ V-(으)ㄹ게요: I will (in spoken language)

	Statement (I will-)
Informal polite	V-(으)ㄹ게요
Casual	V-(으)ㄹ게

❺ V-겠다: I will

	Statement
Formal polite	V-겠습니다
Informal polite	V-겠어요
Casual	V-겠어

REVIEW TEST CHAPTER 6

A Choose the option that has a different meaning from the others.

① 집에 가고 싶어요.

② 집에 갈래요.

③ 집에 갈 수 있어요.

④ 집에 갔으면 좋겠어요.

B Choose the option that is paired with the correct answers.

민호: 이번 주말에 뭐 (   )?

제니: 저는 자전거 (   ).

① 할래요 - 타을래요   ② 핼래요 - 타을래요

③ 핼래요 - 탈래요   ④ 할래요 - 탈래요

C Choose the incorrect sentence.

① 비가 안 왔으면 좋겠어요.

② 집이 더 가까웠으면 좋겠어요.

③ 날씨가 좋았으면 좋겠어요.

④ 영어를 잘 했으면 좋겠어요.

D Choose dialogue that does not make sense.

① A: 전화번호를 알려줄래요?
   B: 네, 여기 쓸게요.

② A: 내일 뭐 할래요?
   B: 저는 영화 보고 싶어요.

③ A: 배가 많이 고파요.
   B: 그럼 밥 먹지 마요.

④ A: 저희 집으로 와 주세요.
   B: 네, 이따가 갈게요.

E In the following dialogue, choose the option that is written incorrectly.

A: 오늘 도서관에서 ①공부할래요?

B: 네, 좋아요.

A: 그런데 저 슈퍼에서 물 좀 ②살게요.

   슈퍼 같이 ③갈래요?

B: 아니요, 저는 도서관에 ④있으게요.

F Choose the sentence where the underlined word is correct.

① 제가 불고기를 만들을게요.

② 한국에서 살으면 좋겠어요.

③ 혼자 음악을 듣고 싶어요.

④ 제가 친구를 도우겠어요.

G Read the following dialogue and choose the incorrect statement.

민호: 수지 씨, 뭐 먹고 싶어요?

수지: 음, 저는 김치찌개 먹을래요.
       민호 씨는요?

민호: 저는 비빔밥이요.
       음료수는 뭐 마실 거예요?

수지: 저는 사과 주스 마실게요.

민호: 네, 그럼 제가 시킬게요.

수지: 맛있었으면 좋겠어요!

① 민호와 수지는 한국 식당에 있습니다.

② 민호는 비빔밥을 먹을 것입니다.

③ 수지는 김치찌개와 포도 주스를 골랐습니다.

④ 민호가 음식을 시킵니다.

🎧 06-V.mp3

No.	✓	Word	Meaning	No.	✓	Word	Meaning
1	☐	비		26	☐	연락하다	
2	☐	혼자		27	☐	초콜릿	
3	☐	돌아가다		28	☐	태국	
4	☐	기숙사		29	☐	차	
5	☐	딸기		30	☐	지키다	
6	☐	꼭		31	☐	반지	
7	☐	소포		32	☐	다이어트	
8	☐	끝내다		33	☐	반	
9	☐	가지다		34	☐	계획	
10	☐	시작하다		35	☐	포도	
11	☐	모임		36	☐	내려가다	
12	☐	못하다		37	☐	물어보다	
13	☐	약하다		38	☐	눕다	
14	☐	다녀오다		39	☐	약속	
15	☐	불다		40	☐	부탁하다	
16	☐	장소		41	☐	시청	
17	☐	데려오다		42	☐	티셔츠	
18	☐	떠나다		43	☐	날씬하다	
19	☐	흰색		44	☐	설탕	
20	☐	처음		45	☐	가깝다	
21	☐	이야기하다		46	☐	강하다	
22	☐	등산하다		47	☐	바람	
23	☐	몸		48	☐	아파트	
24	☐	귤		49	☐	구경하다	
25	☐	여러분		50	☐	준비하다	

Number of words I've learned: _____ / 50

Korea's Beloved Traditional Beverages, Makgeolli and Soju

Makgeolli and Soju are the most beloved and commonly consumed traditional alcoholic beverages in Korea. Let's learn more about these two drinks!

막걸리 Makgeolli

Makgeolli, a rice-based beverage, is known for its low alcohol content, light and subtle flavor, and slight fizziness. This refreshing drink is popular across various age groups. It pairs well with traditional dishes like egg rolls, tofu kimchi, and is especially famous when enjoyed with 파전(pajeon) on rainy days.

소주 Soju

Originally, the word 소주(Soju) referred to the traditional Korean soju, made by distilling cheongju, yakju, or takju. In the old days, since rice, the main ingredient for making alcohol, was scarce, it naturally became very precious. During the Joseon Dynasty, there were frequent measures to prohibit the making of soju due to concerns about food shortages. Distilled soju is still notably more expensive than modern diluted soju.

In the 1960s and 70s, the term 소주(Soju) changed, triggered by the growing popularity of modern, diluted soju. Diluted soju, made from cassava or similar ingredients, is one of the most popularly consumed liquors in modern Korea. Soju, often considered Korea's most popular liquor, is often used as the standard measurement for drinking. It's commonly enjoyed with dishes like 삼겹살(grilled pork belly) or seafood. Additionally, soju is widely used in mixed drinks, with the soju-beer combination known as 소맥(somaek) being particularly famous.

Different regions have their own brands of soju, a result of an implicit agreement to respect each other's territories to prevent territorial disputes. Exploring the variety of soju brands while traveling can provide a unique experience for those interested in Korean culinary culture.

CHAPTER 7
Making Suggestions

UNIT 1   V-(으)ㅂ시다, V-아/어요, V-자 (let's)

UNIT 2   V-(으)ㄹ까요? (shall we/I?)

UNIT 3   V-(으)시겠어요? (would you like to?)

⊙ What you'll learn in this chapter

This chapter teaches you how to politely suggest ideas, activities, or plans during social interactions. You'll learn different ways to invite others or propose actions, using phrases like 'let's do something,' 'shall we,' or asking if someone is willing to participate. Knowing these expressions is important for polite and cooperative communication.

🎧 07-01G.mp3

우리 다 같이 사진 찍읍시다.	여기에서 좀 쉬자.
Let's all take a photo together.	Let's take a break here.

❶ V-(으)ㅂ시다 [(eu)p·si·da] : **Let's (formal polite)**[1]

▸ -(으)ㅂ시다 is used to make polite suggestions or proposals, often among a group in formal situations.

모두 자리에 앉읍시다.	Let's all take our seats.
이제 집에 갑시다.	Let's go home now.

❷ V-아/어요 [a/eo·yo] : **Let's (informal polite)**

▸ The verb ending -아/어요 can also be used to make suggestions, but it's a bit less formal than -(으)ㅂ시다.

저랑 같이 영화 봐요.	Let's watch a movie together with me.
다음 주에 같이 인천에 가요.	Let's go to Incheon together next week.

❸ V-자 [ja] : **Let's (casual)**[2]

▸ -자 is a casual and concise way to make suggestions. It's used in informal settings, such as among close friends or family members.

이따가 카페에서 커피 마시자.	Let's have coffee at the cafe later.
수박 먹자.	Let's eat watermelon.

	Positive (Let's)	Negative (Let's not)[3]
Formal Polite	V-(으)ㅂ시다 [eup·si·da] 먹읍시다 / 마십시다	V-지 맙시다 [ji map·si·da] 먹지 맙시다 / 마시지 맙시다
Informal Polite	V-아/어요 [a/eo·yo] 가요 / 마셔요 / 해요	V-지 마요 [ji ma·yo] 가지 마요 / 마시지 마요 / 하지 마요
Casual	V-자 [ja] 먹자 / 마시자	V-지 말자 [ji mal·ja] 먹지 말자 / 마시지 말자

[1] If the stem ends in a consonant → stem + 읍시다
앉다 → 앉읍시다
If the stem ends in a vowel → stem + ㅂ시다
가다 → 갑시다

[1] -(으)ㅂ시다 is formal but unsuitable for addressing seniors or superiors. Use 같이 V (으)세요 instead.
When addressing someone older of of higher status:
같이 식당에 갑시다. (X)
같이 식당에 가세요. (O)
Let's go to the restaurant together.

[2] It's irrelevant whether the verb stem is a consonant or a vowel → stem + 자
먹다 → 먹자, 마시다 → 마시자

[3] V-지 맙시다, V-지 마요, and V-지 말자 are used to suggest not doing something together.

WORDS

다 [da] all, everything	모두 [mo·du] everyone, everything	자리 [ja·ri] seat, place
이제 [i·je] now	인천 [in·cheon] Incheon	수박 [su·bak] watermelon

Master Grammar By Practicing!

🎧 07-01P.mp3

A Change the given verb to complete the sentence, using '-(으)ㅂ시다'.

공부하다 (to study)	→	이제 모두 <u>공부합시다</u>.

1. 축하하다 (to congratulate) → 영수 씨의 결혼을 _____
2. 먹다 (to eat) → 우리 같이 점심을 _____
3. 타다 (to take) → 지하철을 _____
4. 달리다 (to run) → 저기까지 같이 _____

B Change the underlined verb into 'Let's' form, according to all levels of speech.

백화점 건물 앞에서 <u>만나다</u>.	→	<u>만납시다 / 만나요 / 만나자</u>

1. 할머니 생신 파티에 <u>가다</u>. → _____ / _____ / _____
2. 주말에 다 같이 <u>등산하다</u>. → _____ / _____ / _____
3. 영어 스터디 모임을 <u>만들다</u>. → _____ / _____ / _____
4. 열 시에 <u>출발하다</u>. → _____ / _____ / _____

C Change the underlined verb into 'Let's not' form, corresponding to the level of formality.

주말에 영화를 <u>봅시다</u>.	→	주말에 영화를 <u>보지 맙시다</u>.

1. 우리 택시 <u>타요</u>. → 우리 택시 _____
2. 우리 <u>헤어지자</u>. → 우리 _____
3. 교실에 <u>들어갑시다</u>. → 교실에 _____
4. 주말에 맥주 <u>마시자</u>. → 주말에 맥주 _____

축하하다 [chuk·ha·ha·da] to congratulate **결혼** [gyeol·hon] marriage
달리다 [dal·li·da] to run **건물** [geon·mul] building **출발하다** [chul·bal·ha·da] to depart
헤어지다 [he·eo·ji·da] to part, to break up **맥주** [maek·ju] beer

🎧 07-02G.mp3

이번 주말에 여행갈까요?
Shall we go on a trip this weekend?

라디오를 켤까요?
Shall I turn on the radio?

❶ V-(으)ㄹ까요? [(eu)l·kka·yo] : **Shall we/I?**

▶ -(으)ㄹ까요? is used when the speaker wants to suggest or propose doing something in the form of a question.

▶ -(으)ㄹ까요? is also used to ask about the listener's preference or opinion.

▶ It's similar to "Shall we...?" or "Shall I...?" in English.

❷ Rules

If the stem ends in a consonant	→ Stem + 을까요?	
먹다 (to eat) → 먹 + 을까요?	→ 먹을까요?	
If the stem ends in a vowel or ㄹ	→ Stem + ㄹ까요?	
보다 (to see) → 볼 + ㄹ까요?	→ 볼까요?	
살다 (to live) → 살 + ㄹ까요?	→ 살까요?	

A: 같이 영화 볼까요?
B: 네, 좋아요.

Shall we watch a movie together?
Yes, it sounds good.

A: 저녁으로[1] 뭐 먹을까요?
B: 된장찌개 먹어요.

What shall we have for dinner?
Let's eat doenjang-jjigae.

A: 제가 날짜를 정할까요?
B: 네, 정해 주세요.

Shall I decide the date?
Yes, please decide.

A: 무슨 과일 줄까?
B: 나는 감 먹을래.

What fruit shall I give you?
I'll have a persimmon.

[1] When the particle 으로 is used with food, it translates to 'for' in English, specifying the meal that the food is intended for.

WORDS

라디오 [ra·di·o] radio
된장찌개 [doen·jang·jji·gae] soybean paste stew
날짜 [nal·jja] date
정하다 [jeong·ha·da] to decide
감 [gam] persimmon

Master Grammar By Practicing!

🎧 07-02P.mp3

A Change the given verb to complete the sentence using '-(으)ㄹ까요?'.

(수영하다) Shall we swim...?	→	주말마다 같이 <u>수영할까요?</u>

1. (시키다) Shall we order...? → 김치찌개랑 비빔밥을 _____

2. (타다) Shall we take...? → 배를 _____ 아니면 비행기를 _____

3. (걷다) Shall we walk...? → 공원에서 같이 _____

4. (여행가다) Shall we go on a trip...? → 일본으로 _____

B Change the given verb to complete the sentence using '-(으)ㄹ까요?'.

(기다리다) Shall I wait...?	→	역에서 <u>기다릴까요?</u>

1. (내리다) Shall I unload...? → 자동차에서 짐을 _____

2. (입다) Shall I wear...? → 보라색 스커트를 _____

3. (드리다) Shall I give...? → 맥주를 병으로 _____

4. (건너가다) Shall I cross..? → 건너편으로 _____

C Choose the appropriate verb and complete the conversation using '-(으)ㄹ까요?'.

만나다   사다   시작하다   걸다   놓다

A: 오늘 오후에 회의가 있어요?	B: 네, 있어요. 회의를 언제 <u>시작할까요?</u>

1. A: 어디에서 비행기 표를 _____ B: 여행사에서 사요.

2. A: 짐을 어디에 _____ B: 책상 위에 놔주세요.

3. A: 벽에 뭘 _____ B: 가족 사진을 걸었으면 좋겠어요.

4. A: 몇 시에 _____ B: 두 시에 만나요.

WORDS

배 [bae] ship   역 [yeok] station   짐 [jim] luggage   내리다 [nae·ri·da] to get off, to unload
보라색 [bo·ra·saek] purple   건너편 [geo·nneo·pyeon] opposite side
건너가다 [geon·neo·ga·da] to go across   여행사 [yeo·haeng·sa] travel agency   벽 [byeok] wall

🎧 07-03G.mp3

먼저 나가시겠어요?
Would you like to go out first?

머리¹를 자르시겠어요?
Would you like to get a haircut?

❶ V-(으)시겠어요? [(eu)·si·get·sseo·yo] : **Would you like to?**

▸ -(으)시겠어요?² is for making polite suggestions or inquiries about someone's preference or intention.

▸ It's equivalent to the English phrase 'Would you like/mind to... ?'

❷ Rules

If the stem ends in a consonant	→ Stem + 으시겠어요?	
앉다 (to sit)	→ 앉 + 으시겠어요?	→ 앉으시겠어요?
If the stem ends in a vowel or ㄹ	→ Stem + 시겠어요?	
오다 (to come)	→ 오 + 시겠어요?	→ 오시겠어요?
살다 (to live)	→ 살 + 시겠어요?	→ 사시겠어요?

A: 몇 시에 오시겠어요?   When will you come?
B: 두 시까지 가겠습니다.   I will go by two o'clock.

A: 자리에 앉아 주시겠어요?   Would you mind taking a seat?
B: 네, 앉을게요.   Yes, I will sit down.

❸ Difference between -(으)시겠어요? and -(으)ㄹ래요?

▸ -(으)시겠어요? offers a higher level of formality and politeness compared to the less formal -(으)ㄹ래요? or -(으)실래요?.

저녁 식사 하시겠어요?³   Would you like to have dinner?
저녁 식사 하실래요?⁴   Would you like to have dinner?
저녁 식사 할래요?⁵   Do you want to have dinner?
저녁 식사 할래?⁶   Want to have dinner?

¹머리 translates to 'head' but in Korean, it often refers to 'hair (머리카락)'. When Koreans say 머리, they are usually talking about hair, not the head itself.

² The suffix 시 is commonly used in honorific language, and 겠어요 implies a future or a potential action.

³ Very formal and polite. Suitable for respectful situations or with elders.

⁴ Used with acquaintances or in respectful, yet slightly informal contexts.

⁵ Informal and friendly. Used among peers or people of similar age.

⁶ Very informal and casual. Typically used with close friends or family members.

WORDS

먼저 [meon·jeo] first
머리카락 [meo·ri·ka·rak] hair

자르다 [ja·reu·da] to cut
식사하다 [sik·sa·ha·da] to have a meal

Master Grammar By Practicing!

🎧 07-03P.mp3

A Change the given verb to complete the sentence using '-(으)시겠어요'.

드시다 (to eat)	→	이 음식 좀 <u>드시겠어요?</u>

1. 쉬다 (to rest) → 잠깐 _____
2. 오다 (to come) → 이쪽으로 _____
3. 갈아입다 (to change one's clothes) → 이 옷으로 _____
4. 감다 (to close one's eyes) → 눈을 _____

B Change the '-(으)ㄹ래요?' form into '-(으)시겠어요'.

제 생일 파티에 올래요?	→	제 생일 파티에 <u>오시겠어요?</u>

1. 주소를 여기에 <u>쓸래요?</u> → 주소를 여기에 _____
2. 이 신발 <u>신을래요?</u> → 이 신발 _____
3. 저한테 이유를 <u>말할래요?</u> → 저한테 이유를 _____
4. 오늘은 집에서 <u>쉴래요?</u> → 오늘은 집에서 _____

C Choose the appropriate verb and complete the conversation using '-(으)시겠어요'.

씻다   사다   드시다   보다   가르쳐 주다

A: 우리 뭐 먹을까요?	B: 갈비 <u>드시겠어요?</u>

1. A: 우리 이제 요리 시작해요.   B: 손 먼저 _____
2. A: 이 편지를 프랑스에 보낼 거예요.   B: 우표를 _____
3. A: 한국어 공부하고 있어요?   B: 네, 이 단어 좀 _____
4. A: 주말에 같이 드라마 _____   B: 좋아요, 무슨 드라마 보고 싶어요?

WORDS

잠깐 [jam·kkan] a moment   **이쪽** [i·jjok] this way, this side   **갈아입다** [ga·ra·ip·tta] to change clothes
주소 [ju·so] address   **이유** [i·yu] reason   **갈비** [gal·bi] ribs
손 [son] hand   **우표** [u·pyo] stamp

🎧 07-C.mp3

다니엘: 지수 씨, 봄 날씨가 너무 좋아요. Jisoo, the spring weather is so nice.

우리 주말에 같이 소풍 갈까요? Shall we go on a picnic this weekend?

지수: 네, 좋아요! 어디로 갈까요? Yes, that sounds great! Where shall we go?

다니엘: 남산 갈래요? 거기 꽃이 진짜 예뻐요.
Want to go to Namsan? The flowers there are really beautiful.

지수: 저도 사진에서 봤어요. I saw them in pictures, too.

저도 거기 가고 싶었어요. I wanted to go there as well.

다니엘: 그럼 제가 김밥 만들게요. Then I'll make kimbap.

지수: 다니엘 씨 김밥 만들 줄 알아요? Do you know how to make kimbap?

다니엘: 그럼요! 정말 맛있을 거예요. Of course! It will be really delicious.

지수 씨가 음료수 준비해 주시겠어요? Could you prepare the drinks?

지수: 네, 제가 콜라랑 물 가져갈게요. Yes, I'll bring cola and water.

✎ 그럼요! translates to "Of course!" in English. It's used to positively respond to a question or statement, indicating strong agreement or confirmation.

WORDS　　소풍 [so·pung] picnic　　　　가져가다 [ga·jeo·ga·da] to take (something with you)

RECAP CHAPTER 7

❶ V-(으)ㅂ시다, V-아/어요/ V-자: Let's

	Positive (Let's)	Negative (Let's not)
Formal polite	V-(으)ㅂ시다 앉읍시다 / 갑시다	V-지 맙시다 앉지 맙시다 / 가지 맙시다
Informal Polite	V-아/어요 가요 / 먹어요 / 일해요	V-지 마요 가지 마요 / 먹지 마요 / 일하지 마요
Casual	V-자 앉자 / 가자	V-지 말자 앉지 말자 / 가지 말자

❷ V-(으)ㄹ까요?: Shall we?, Shall I?

If the verb stem ends in a consonant → stem + 을까요?
If the verb stem ends in a vowel → stem + ㄹ까요?

	Question
Informal polite	V-(으)ㄹ까요? 앉을까요? / 갈까요?
Casual	V-(으)ㄹ까? 앉을까? / 갈까?

❸ V-(으)시겠어요?: Would you like to?

Used to make polite suggestions or inquiries about someone's preference or intention.

	Question
Informal polite	V-(으)시겠어요? 앉으시겠어요? / 가시겠어요?

A Choose the option that has a different meaning from the others.

① 다 같이 사진 찍읍시다.

② 다 같이 사진 찍어요.

③ 다 같이 사진 찍을까?

④ 다 같이 사진 찍자.

B Choose the sentence where the underlined word is correct.

① (to change) 이 신발 바꾸을까요?

② (to hang) 벽에 그림을 걸을까요?

③ (to put) 가방에 음료수를 넣을까요?

④ (to cross) 저기로 건너갈까요?

C Choose the incorrect sentence.

① (to transfer) 버스를 갈아타시겠어요?

② (to carry) 가방을 드시겠어요?

③ (to wear shoes) 운동화를 신시겠어요?

④ (to turn on) 불을 켜시겠어요?

D Choose dialogue that does not make sense.

① A: 우리 같이 영화 볼래요?

   B: 네, 무슨 영화 볼까요?

② A: 이 떡 좀 드시겠어요?

   B: 네, 떡을 드릴까요?

③ A: 책을 빌려주시겠어요?

   B: 무슨 책 줄까요?

④ A: 같이 춤 배울래요?

   B: 좋아요. 어디에서 배울까요?

E In the following dialogue, choose the option that is written incorrectly.

> A: 등산 언제 ①할까요?
>
> B: 이번 주 일요일에 ②가웁시다.
>
> A: 저는 일요일에 약속이 있어요.
>
>   다음 일요일에 시간 ③괜찮으시겠어요?
>
> B: 네, 괜찮아요. 그럼 다음 주에 ④만나요.

F Choose the correct option of the underlined verb in the '-자' form.

> 커피 마시다.   여기에 앉다.

① 마시자 - 앉자   ② 마신자 - 앉으자

③ 마시자 - 앉다   ④ 마실자 - 앉으자

G Read the following dialogue and choose the incorrect statement.

> 지수: 파티 준비 같이 할까?
>
> 유나: 응, 고마워. 언제 시간 괜찮아?
>
> 지수: 주말은 다 괜찮아. 토요일에 만날까?
>
> 유나: 응, 좋아. 그럼 학교에서 두 시에 보자.
>
> 지수: 그래. 내가 뭐 가져갈까?
>
> 유나: 물건은 내가 가져갈게.
>
> 지수: 응, 그럼 토요일에 보자.

① 지수와 유나는 파티를 함께 준비합니다.

② 지수의 유나는 토요일에 만납니다.

③ 지수와 유나는 두 시에 학교에서 만납니다.

④ 지수가 물건을 가져올 것입니다.

🎧 07-V.mp3

No.	✓	Word	Meaning	No.	✓	Word	Meaning
1	☐	우표		26	☐	배 (vehicle)	
2	☐	수박		27	☐	이제	
3	☐	벽		28	☐	건물	
4	☐	감		29	☐	된장찌개	
5	☐	날짜		30	☐	이쪽	
6	☐	가져가다		31	☐	보라색	
7	☐	잠깐		32	☐	인천	
8	☐	짐		33	☐	내리다	
9	☐	소풍		34	☐	자르다	
10	☐	건너가다		35	☐	라디오	
11	☐	건너편		36	☐	머리카락	
12	☐	맥주		37	☐	출발하다	
13	☐	정하다		38	☐	손	
14	☐	헤어지다		39	☐	식사하다	
15	☐	여행사		40	☐	모두	
16	☐	갈아입다		41	☐	역	
17	☐	달리다					
18	☐	다					
19	☐	자리					
20	☐	축하하다					
21	☐	갈비					
22	☐	주소					
23	☐	결혼					
24	☐	먼저					
25	☐	이유					

Number of words I've learned: _____ / 41

Exploring the Characteristics of Korean Names

In Korea, names consist of a family name and a given name, with the family name symbolizing the roots and status of the family, which is often inherited over centuries within a single lineage. Koreans typically inherit their ancestors' family names. For example, 김(Kim), 이(Lee), 박(Park) and 최(Choi) are common family names, widely used in Korean society.

A characteristic of Korean names is the small number of family names compared to the abundance of given names. Korea has only about 200 family names. In Korea, people are often referred to by their given names rather than their family names. Unlike other countries, people in Korea usually keep their own surnames after marriage.

Korean names consist of a family name (성 [seong]) followed by a given name (이름 [i·reum]). In a Korean name, the surname comes first, followed by the given name. For example, in the name 김지원(Kim Jiwon), 김(Kim) is the family name, and 지원(Jiwon) is the given name. Modern Korean names typically consist of three syllables: one syllable for the family name and two for the given name.

Korean names usually incorporate meaningful Chinese characters (한자 [han·ja]). When parents choose a name for their child, they select Chinese characters reflecting the child's traits or the family's wishes. These characters often convey positive values or specific meanings, expressing parents' hopes for their child's future.

There are also names without Chinese characters for the given names, known as native Korean names. Native Korean names come in various types, including those derived from concrete nouns (such as 가람 [ga·ram], 하늘 [ha·neul], 잔디 [jan·di]), abstract nouns (such as 보라 [bo·ra], 나라 [na·ra], 누리 [nu·ri]), and adjectives (such as 기쁨 [gi·ppeum], 아름 [ar·eum], 조은 [jo·eun]).

Creating your own unique Korean name by finding a Korean pronunciation similar to your own and assigning it special meanings can be a delightful experience.

CHAPTER 8
Purpose and Decision

What you'll learn in this chapter

In Chapter 8, we focus on how to express purpose and make decisions in Korean. This chapter teaches you to explain why you do something and what your intentions are. You'll explore various structures that convey the reasons behind actions and the decisions regarding future actions. By the end of this chapter, you will be able to effectively communicate your motives and decisions.

UNIT 1
V-(으)러 가다/오다
(to go/come in order to)

🎧 08-01G.mp3

옷을 사러 시장에 갔어요.　　저희 집에 놀러 오세요.
I went to the market to buy clothes.　Please come to our house to hang out.

❶ V-(으)러 가다/오다 [(eu)·reo ga·da/o·da] : **to go/come to**

▶ -(으)러 is used to express the purpose of movement.

▶ Only movement verbs such as 가다 (to go), 오다 (to come), 다니다
   (to attend/commute), 올라가다 (to go up) and 나가다 (to go out) are
   used with -(으)러.

▶ It indicates that the purpose or intention for the movement (the
   second verb) is to accomplish what's described in the first verb.

▶ It is translated as '(move) in order to V'.

❷ Rules

If the stem ends in a consonant	→ Stem + 으러	
먹다 (to eat)	→ 먹 + 으러	→ 먹으러
If the stem ends in a vowel or ㄹ	→ Stem + 러	
자다 (to sleep)	→ 자 + 러	→ 자러
살다 (to live)	→ 살 + 러	→ 살러

소고기 먹으러 식당에 갈 거예요.　We're going to the restaurant to eat beef.

엄마는 방금 방에 자러 갔어요.　My mom just went to the room to sleep.

저희 집에 식사하러 오세요.　Please come to our house to have a meal.

시험 준비하러 도서관에 가요.　I go to the library to prepare for the exam.

커피 마시러 나갈까요?　Shall we go out to drink coffee?

과자 먹으러 내려오세요.　Please come down to eat snacks.

WORDS

소고기 [so·go·gi] beef　　**방금** [bang·geum] just (now), a moment ago

과자 [gwa·ja] snack　　**내려오다** [nae·ryeo·o·da] to come down

Master Grammar By Practicing!

A Change the given verb to complete the sentence using '-(으)러 가다/오다'.

🎧 08-01P.mp3

만나다 (to meet)	→	친구 <u>만나러</u> 카페에 가요.

1. 낚시하다 (to fish) → ＿＿＿＿＿＿＿ 호수에 갈까요?

2. 돕다 (to help) → 친구를 ＿＿＿＿＿＿＿ 친구 집에 왔어요.

3. 인사하다 (to greet) → 할아버지와 할머니께 ＿＿＿＿＿＿＿ 갔어요.

4. 팔다 (to sell) → 옷을 ＿＿＿＿＿＿＿시장에 갈 거예요.

B Look at the pictures and answer the question, matching the tense and the level of formality of the question.

 꽃집　　 스키장　　 서점　　 미술관　　 마트

(사다)	A: 어디에 가요?	B: 책을 <u>사러 서점에 가요.</u>

1. (보다) A: 어디에 가요? B: 그림을 ＿＿＿＿＿＿＿＿＿＿＿

2. (사다) A: 엄마는 어디 갔어? B: 꽃을 ＿＿＿＿＿＿＿＿＿＿＿

3. (타다) A: 어제 어디에 갔어요? B: 스키를 ＿＿＿＿＿＿＿＿＿＿＿

4. (사다) A: 어디 가? B: 우유를 ＿＿＿＿＿＿＿＿＿＿＿

C Match objects, verbs in '(으)러' form, and locations to complete the sentence.

1. 책을　　　　　　a. 사다 → ＿＿＿＿＿　　　가. 은행에 가요.

2. 기차를　　　　　b. 찾다 → ＿＿＿＿＿　　　나. 도서관에 가요.

3. 빵을　　　　　　c. 빌리다 → <u>빌리러</u>　　다. 빵집에 가요.

4. 밥을　　　　　　d. 타다 → ＿＿＿＿＿　　　라. 식당에 가요.

5. 돈을　　　　　　e. 먹다 → ＿＿＿＿＿　　　마. 기차역에 가요.

WORDS

낚시하다 [nak·si·ha·da] to fish	**호수** [ho·su] lake	**인사하다** [in·sa·ha·da] to greet
미술관 [mi·sul·gwan] art gallery	**꽃집** [kkot·jip] flower shop	**스키장** [seu·ki·jang] ski resort
마트 [ma·teu] mart	**기차역** [gi·cha·yeok] train station	**빵집** [ppang·jip] bakery

| **V-(으)려고 (in order to)**

🎧 08-02G.mp3

친구를 사귀려고 모임에 나갔어요.
I went to a club to make friends.

요리사가 되려고 전공을 바꿨어요.
I changed my major to become a cook.

❶ V-(으)려고¹ [(eu)·ryeo·go] : in order to

▶ -(으)려고 is used to express a speaker's intention or purpose to do something. It indicates that the purpose or reason for doing the second action is to accomplish what's described in the first verb.

▶ It can be used with all verbs, including movement verbs.

A: 왜² 다이어트를 해요?   Why do you go on a diet?
B: 이 옷을 입으려고 다이어트하고 있어요.   I am dieting to wear this outfit.

❷ Difference between -(으)러 and -(으)려고

▶ -(으)러 focuses more on the fact of going or coming, while -(으)려고 emphasizes the purpose or reason for the action.

책을 사러 서점에 가요.³   책을 사려고 서점에 가요.⁴

▶ -(으)러 can only be used with movement verbs such as '오다' (to come) and '가다' (to go), while -(으)려고 can be used with any verb.

with movement verb

책을 사러 서점에 <u>가요</u>. (O)
책을 사려고 서점에 <u>가요</u>. (O)

with other verb

책을 사러 돈을 <u>모아요</u>. (X)
책을 사려고 돈을 <u>모아요</u>. (O)

▶ -(으)러 can be used in all tenses and sentence forms, but -(으)려고 cannot be used in future tense and sentences that involve making a request to do something together.

Future Tense

책 사러 서점에 <u>갈 거예요</u>. (O)
책 사려고 서점에 <u>갈 거예요</u>. (X)

Making a request

책 사러 서점에 <u>갈래요?</u> (O)
책 사려고 서점에 <u>갈래요?</u> (X)

¹ If the stem ends in a consonant → stem + 으려고
입다 → 입으려고
If the stem ends in a vowel or ㄹ → stem + 려고
사다 → 사려고
만들다 → 만들려고

² 왜 is an interrogative word meaning 'why'.

³ This emphasizes the action of going to the bookstore with the purpose of buying a book.

⁴ This emphasizes the intention of buying a book, rather than just the act of going to the bookstore.

WORDS   요리사 [yo·ri·sa] cook, chef   전공 [jeon·gong] major (field of study)   모으다 [mo·eu·da] to gather

Master Grammar By Practicing!

🎧 08-02P.mp3

A Change the given verb to complete the sentence using '-(으)려고'.

공부하다 (to study)	→	영어 공부하려고 책을 또 샀어요.

1. 쉬다 (to rest) → 이제 좀 _____ 여행을 계획하고 있어요.
2. 찾아보다 (to look up) → 단어를 _____ 사전을 샀어요.
3. 고치다 (to repair) → 핸드폰을 _____ 애플 스토어에 들렀어요.
4. 씻다 (to wash) → 손을 _____ 화장실에 갔어요.

B Answer the question with the given verb, matching the tense and the level of formality of the question.

(만나다)	A: 영국에 왜 가요?	B: 부모님을 만나려고 가요.

1. (배우다) A: 이 책을 왜 읽어요? B: 한국 역사를 _____
2. (같이 먹다) A: 케이크를 왜 만들었어요? B: 남편이랑 _____
3. (알려 주다) A: 아까 왜 전화했어요? B: 시험 날짜를 _____
4. (사다) A: 오늘 왜 마트에 들렀어요? B: 과일을 _____

C Correct the underlined verb, in case it is incorrect.

여행을 하러 기차표를 샀어요. (correct / incorrect)	→	하려고

1. 약을 사러 약국에 갈 거예요. (correct / incorrect) → _____
2. 조용히 공부하러 문을 닫았어요. (correct / incorrect) → _____
3. 친구가 밥 먹으려고 여기 올 거예요. (correct / incorrect) → _____
4. 살 빼려고 매일 운동을 해요. (correct / incorrect) → _____

WORDS	또 [tto] again	찾아보다 [cha·ja·bo·da] to look up, to search	사전 [sa·jeon] dictionary
	고치다 [go·chi·da] to repair	들르다 [deul·reu·da] to stop by	화장실 [hwa·jang·sil] restroom
	역사 [yeok·sa] history	살 [sal] fat	빼다 [ppae·da] to remove, to lose weight

UNIT 3
V-(으)려고 하다 (to plan to)
V-기로 하다 (to decide to)

🎧 08-03G.mp3

주말에 여자친구랑 데이트하려고 해요.
I plan to go on a date with
my girlfriend this weekend.

올해부터 술을 끊기로 했어요.
I decided to quit drinking
from this year

❶ V- (으)려고 하다¹ [(eu)·ryeo·go ha·da]: **to plan to**

▶ -(으)려고 하다 is used to indicate the speaker's intention or plan to do something in the near future.

　내일 친구를 만나려고 해요.　I plan to meet my friend tomorrow.

❷ V-기로 하다² [gi·ro ha·da]: **to decide to**

▶ -기로 하다 is used for decisions made by oneself, essentially a promise or resolution to oneself.

　한국어를 배우기로 했어요.　I decided to learn Korean.

▶ -기로 하다 is used when an agreement or promise is made with another person.

　내일 친구를 만나기로 했어요.　My friend and I promised to meet tomorrow.

❸ Difference between - (으)려고 하다 and -기로 하다

▶ -(으)려고 하다 is more about intention or a tentative plan, whereas -기로 하다 indicates a firm decision or agreement.

▶ -(으)려고 하다 corresponds with the present tense³ as it expresses current intentions or plans, while -기로 하다 is often used in the past tense to indicate decisions or agreements that have already been made.

　제 방 창문을 닦으려고 해요. I plan to clean my room's window.
　→ I'm planning to clean my room's window in the future.

　우리는 매주 회의하기로 했어요. We decided to have meetings every week.
　→ The decision to have weekly meetings was made in the past.

¹ If the stem ends in a consonant
→ stem + 으려고 하다
If the stem ends in a vowel or ㄹ
→ stem + 려고 하다

² It's irrelevant whether the stem ends in a consonant or a vowel → stem + 기로 하다

³ When -(으)려고 하다 is used in the past tense, it indicates a past intention or plan that may not have been realized.
오늘 책을 읽으려고 했어요.
I had planned to read a book today.
→ the speaker had the intention to read a book, but this plan did not happen.

WORDS　　데이트하다 [de·i·teu·ha·da] to go on a date　　끊다 [kkeun·tta] to quit　　닦다 [dak·tta] to clean, to wipe

Master Grammar By Practicing!

A Choose the appropriate word and complete the question '-(으)려고 해요'.

🎧 08-03P.mp3

걷다   버리다   초대하다   일하다   쉬다

> A: 이번 생일에 뭐 할 거예요?   B: 친구들을 집에 <u>초대하려고 해요</u>.

1. A: 곧 졸업이에요. 뭐 할 거예요?   B: 회사에서 _____
2. A: 주말에 뭐 해요?   B: 공원에서 좀 _____
3. A: 이번 휴가에 뭐 할 거예요?   B: 집에서 조용히 _____
4. A: 이 카메라 계속 쓸 거예요?   B: 아니요, _____

B Choose the appropriate word and complete the question using '-기로 했어요'.

쓰다   치다   예약하다   끊다   가져오다

> 학교 콘서트를 할 거예요. 요코가 피아노를 <u>치기로 했어요</u>.

1. 저는 새해 계획이 있어요. 올해에는 담배를 꼭 _____
2. 졸업 파티를 함께 준비하고 있어요. 지수랑 헨리가 음료수를 _____
3. 한국어를 잘하고 싶어요. 그래서 매일 한국어로 일기를 _____
4. 그 식당에는 사람이 많아요. 그래서 미리 _____

C Choose whether to use '-(으)려고' or '-기로' for the blank.

> 가다 (to go)   →   동생은 내일 병원에 <u>가려고</u> 해요.

1. 여행가다 (to go on a trip)   →   이번 여름 휴가에 멀리 _____ 해요.
2. 잊다 (to forget)   →   지금부터 남자친구는 _____ 했어요.
3. 시작하다 (to start)   →   내일부터 다이어트를 _____ 했어요.
4. 바꾸다 (to change)   →   내년에 대학 전공을 _____ 해요.

WORDS

곧 [got] soon
새해 [sae·hae] New Year
예약하다 [ye·yak·ha·da] to reserve

졸업 [jo·reop] graduation
일기 [il·gi] diary
멀리 [meol·li] far away

조용히 [jo·yong·hi] quietly
미리 [mi·ri] in advance
잊다 [it·tta] to forget

08-04G.mp3

사람들이 지나가게 문을 잡아 주세요.
Please hold the door so that people pass by.

걱정하지 않게 자주 전화해요.
Call me often so that I don't worry.

❶ V-게 [ge] : so that

▶ -게 is used to indicate the purpose of the action that follows.

▶ The clause following '-게' provides the conditions or methods to achieve the situation described in the preceding clause.

❷ Rules

> Stem + 게
>
> 먹다 (to eat) → 먹게   가다 (to go) → 가게

약을 먹게 물을 주세요.
Please give me some water so that I can take the medicine.

❸ Differences between –게 and –(으)려고

▶ -게 is typically used when the subject of the preceding and following clauses differ.
<u>아기가</u> 잘 수 있게 <u>우리는</u> 조용히 말했어요.[1]
We spoke quietly so that the baby could sleep.

▶ -게 can be used in sentences that make requests or give commands, whereas –(으)려고 하다 cannot be used in such sentences.[2]

드라마 보게 텔레비전을 켜 주세요. (O)
Please turn on the television so that I can watch the drama.

드라마 <u>보려고</u> 텔레비전을 켜 주세요. (X)

[1] In the -게 form, the verb is not used in the past tense. Therefore, 잘 수 있었게 is incorrect.

[2] -게 is used when the subjects of connected clauses differ, making it suitable for requests or commands where the subject is 'you'.

WORDS
지나가다 [ji·na·ga·da] to pass by   잡다 [jab·tta] to grab, to catch
걱정하다 [geok·jeong·ha·da] to worry

Master Grammar By Practicing!

🎧 08-04P.mp3

A Change the given verb to complete the sentence using '-게'.

공부하다 (to study)	→	학생들이 공부하게 조용히 해 주십시오.

1. 주문하다 (to order) → _____ 메뉴를 주세요.

2. 넘어지지 않다 (to not fall down) → _____ 조심하세요.

3. 따뜻하다 (to be warm) → 엄마가 _____ 차를 드렸어요.

4. 사다 (to buy) → 과일을 _____ 돈을 주세요.

B Choose the appropriate word and complete the sentence, using '-(으)ㄹ 수 있게'.

보다   먹다   쉬다   끊다   앉다

할아버지가 쉴 수 있게 모두 나가 주세요.

1. 시험을 잘 _____ 도와주세요.   2. 할머니가 _____ 의자를 가져왔어요.

3. 같이 _____ 그릇을 하나 더 주세요.   4. 담배를 _____ 껌을 씹으세요.

C Combine the given two sentences into one sentence, using '-게'.

아이들이 먹을 수 있어요. 고추장을 조금만 넣어 주세요.
→ 아이들이 먹을 수 있게 고추장을 조금만 넣어 주세요.

1. 연필을 써요. 깎아 주세요.   → _____

2. 살을 뺄 수 있어요. 헬스클럽에 다녀요.   → _____

3. 실수하지 않아요. 열심히 준비하세요.   → _____

4. 잘 볼 수 있어요. 불을 켜 주세요.   → _____

WORDS

주문하다 [ju·mun·ha·da] to order (items or food)   **넘어지다** [neo·meo·ji·da] to fall down
조심하다 [jo·sim·ha·da] to be careful   **껌** [kkeom] gum   **씹다** [ssip·tta] to chew
고추장 [go·chu·jang] red chili paste   **깎다** [kkak·tta] to peel, to cut
헬스클럽 [hel·seu·keul·leop] gym, health club   **실수하다** [sil·su·ha·da] to make a mistake

🎧 08-C.mp3

요코: 헨리 씨, 어디 가요? Henry, where are you going?

헨리: 저 책 사러 서점에 가요. I'm going to the bookstore to buy a book.

요코: 무슨 책 사려고요? What book are you going to buy?

헨리: 한국어 책 사려고 해요. I'm going to buy a Korean book.

저 이제 공부 열심히 하기로 했어요. I've decided to study hard now.

요코: 한국어 연습할 수 있게 학원 다니지 않을래요?
Don't you want to attend a language school to practice Korean?

헨리: 네, 학원에도 다니고 싶어요. Yes, I also want to attend a language school.

어느 학원이 좋아요? 좀 알려주세요. Which one is good? Please let me know.

요코: 저는 토미 학원에 다니고 있어요. I'm attending Tomi School.

수업 보러 한번 오세요. Come to see a class once.

헨리: 네, 다음에 갈게요. Yes, I'll go next time.

✏️ -(으)려고 하다 can be shortened to V-(으)려고요 (polite) or V-(으)려고 (casual) and used as a sentence ending to express plans to do something.

✏️ In Korea, a 학원 is a private educational institute where students attend additional classes beyond regular school hours.

WORDS 학원 [ha·gwon] private academy

RECAP CHAPTER 8

❶ V-(으)러 and V-(으)려고: in order to

-(으)러	-(으)려고
Only used with movement verbs 공부하러 학교에 가요. (O) 공부하러 책을 사요. (X)	Used with any verb 공부하려고 학교에 가요. (O) 공부하려고 책을 사요. (O)
Focuses more on the fact of the movement 공부하러 학교에 가요. → Going to school is more important	Emphasizes the purpose or reason 공부하려고 학교에 가요. → The reason 'to study' is more important.
Used in all tenses and sentence forms 공부하러 학교에 갈 거예요. (O) 공부하러 학교에 갈까요? (O) 공부하러 학교에 가세요. (O)	Awkward when used with the future tense or in request and command sentences 공부하려고 학교에 갈 거예요. (X) 공부하려고 학교에 갈까요? (X)

❷ V-(으)려고 하다: to plan to, V-기로 하다: to decide to

-(으)려고 하다	-기로 하다
Indicates the speaker's intention or plan to do something in the future 주말에 공부하려고 해요. → plan to study	Indicates the speaker's decision, essentially resolution to oneself. 주말에 공부하기로 했어요. → decided to study
Typically used with the present tense 한국어를 배우려고 해요.	Typically used with the present tense 한국어를 배우기로 했어요.

❸ V-게: so that

-게	-(으)려고
Used when the subjects of two clauses are different 아이가 물을 마실 수 있게 엄마가 컵을 주었어요.	Used when the subjects of two clauses are the same 아이가 물을 마시려고 컵을 가져왔어요.
Can be used in request and command sentences 물을 마시게 컵을 주세요. (O)	Cannot be used in request and command sentences 물을 마시려고 컵을 주세요. (X)

REVIEW TEST CHAPTER 8

A Choose the correct option of the underlined verb in the '-(으)려고' form.

> 술을 <u>끊다</u> 약을 먹고 있어요.
> 살을 <u>빼다</u> 운동하고 있어요.

① 끊을려고 - 빼으려고
② 끊으려고 - 빼려고
③ 끊으려고 - 뺄려고
④ 끊을려고 - 빼려고

B Choose the sentence where the underlined word is **incorrect**.

① <u>공부하게</u> 조용히 해주세요.
② 한국어를 <u>배우려고</u> 책을 주세요.
③ 책을 <u>사러</u> 서점에 갔어요.
④ 저희 집에 <u>식사하러</u> 오세요.

C Choose the sentence that does **not** make sense.

① 케이크를 만들려고 우유를 샀어요.
② 그림을 보러 헬스클럽에 갔어요.
③ 낚시를 하려고 호수에 갔어요
④ 소풍 가려고 음식을 준비했어요.

D Choose the option that is paired with the correct answers.

> A: 겨울 방학에 뭐 할 거예요?
> B: 중국어를 (   ) 해요.
> A: 중국어를 어떻게 배울 거예요?
> B: 학원에 (   ) 했어요.

① 배우기로 - 다니기로   ② 배우기로 - 다니려고
③ 배우려고 - 다니기로   ④ 배우려고 - 다니려고

E In the following passage, choose the option that is written **incorrectly**.

> 친구가 결혼을 했어요. 그래서 ①<u>축하할려고</u> 친구에게 전화했어요. 친구에게 선물도 ②<u>주려고</u> 해요. 그림을 ③<u>선물하기로</u> 했어요. 그림을 ④<u>사러</u> 백화점에 갈 거예요.

F Choose the correct sentence.

① 10층에 가려고 엘리베이터를 탔어요.
② 혼자 공부하려고 책을 사세요.
③ 커피 마시게 카페에 갔어요?
④ 친구랑 먹으러 초콜릿을 샀어요.

G Read the following dialogue and choose the **incorrect** statement.

> 제니: 민호 씨 이번 생일에 뭐 할 거예요?
> 민호: 이번에는 조용히 보내려고 해요.
> 제니: 왜요? 생일 파티 안 해요?
> 민호: 네, 좀 쉬러 혼자 여행가기로 했어요.
> 제니: 그럼 저는 민호 씨가 쉴 수 있게 다음에 축하할게요. 여행 잘 다녀오세요.
> 민호: 네, 고마워요.

① 제니가 민호의 생일 계획을 묻습니다.
② 민호는 생일 파티를 안 하기로 했습니다.
③ 민호는 혼자 여행을 갑니다.
④ 제니는 민호의 생일을 축하했습니다.

🎧 08-V.mp3

No.	✓	Word	Meaning	No.	✓	Word	Meaning
1	☐	씹다		26	☐	고치다	
2	☐	끊다		27	☐	내려오다	
3	☐	호수		28	☐	미리	
4	☐	마트		29	☐	조용히	
5	☐	낚시하다		30	☐	헬스클럽	
6	☐	소고기		31	☐	빵집	
7	☐	조심하다		32	☐	기차역	
8	☐	곧		33	☐	요리사	
9	☐	사전		34	☐	예약하다	
10	☐	과자		35	☐	닦다	
11	☐	멀리		36	☐	방금	
12	☐	전공		37	☐	빼다	
13	☐	잊다		38	☐	실수하다	
14	☐	지나가다		39	☐	역사	
15	☐	넘어지다		40	☐	화장실	
16	☐	일기		41	☐	주문하다	
17	☐	찾아보다		42	☐	미술관	
18	☐	데이트하다		43	☐	인사하다	
19	☐	새해		44	☐	살	
20	☐	모으다		45	☐	학원	
21	☐	스키장		46	☐	들르다	
22	☐	또		47	☐	걱정하다	
23	☐	꽃집		48	☐	잡다	
24	☐	고추장		49	☐	깎다	
25	☐	졸업		50	☐	껌	

Number of words I've learned: _____ / 50

The Most Popular Tourist Destination in Korea - Jeju Island

Jeju Island, located in the south of South Korea, is the largest island in the country and a favorite destination among Koreans and international travelers alike. Let's explore the captivating charm of Jeju Island.

Jeju Island covers an area of 1,833.2 square kilometers, with a population of approximately 700,000. Formed by volcanic activity, Jeju Island boasts beautiful landscapes and diverse terrain as a result of volcanic eruptions. At the center of the island lies Hallasan, the highest mountain on the Korean Peninsula and one of the distinctive geographical features of Jeju Island. Jeju Island is renowned for its stunning beaches, with the coast particularly popular for beach resorts due to its clear waters.

성산 일출봉 Seongsan Ilchulbong
Known for offering the most beautiful sunrise views on Jeju Island, Seongsan Ilchulbong is located on the coast and is recognized as one of Korea's natural landscapes. It is also listed as a UNESCO World Natural Heritage site.

한라산 Hallasan (Halla Mountain)

As the highest peak on Jeju Island and in South Korea at 1,950 meters, Mount Hallasan is extremely popular among hikers. Various trails offer visitors magnificent views from the summit.

정방 폭포 Jeongbang Waterfall
This waterfall is one of the few in Asia that falls directly into the ocean. The scenic beauty of Jeongbang Waterfall, surrounded by lush vegetation and the ocean backdrop, makes it a popular spot for both tourists and locals.

CHAPTER 9
Connecting Sentences

ⓞ What you'll learn in this chapter

In Chapter 9, we explore how to connect sentences in Korean using a variety of connectors. You'll learn to link thoughts with conjunctions like 'and', 'then', 'or', and 'but', and understand the nuances they add to sentences. Mastering these will help you express complex ideas and improve your conversational flow. By the end of this chapter, you will be better equipped to create clear and detailed conversations in Korean.

UNIT 1 | A/V-고 (and)

09-01G.mp3

저는 학생이고 민지는 간호사예요.
I am a student and Minji is a nurse.

저는 요리를 하고 다니엘은 청소를 했어요.
I cooked, and Daniel cleaned.

❶ A/V-고[go] : and

▶ -고 is a connective ending used to connect two or more clauses.

❷ Rules

Stem + 고		
가다 (to go) → 가고	먹다 (to eat) → 먹고
예쁘다 (to be pretty) → 예쁘고	덥다 (to be hot) → 덥고

1) It's used to list of actions or states: and

저는 스무 살이에요. 그리고 여동생은 열여덟 살이에요.
I am twenty years old. And my sister is eighteen years old.

→ 저는 스무 살이고 여동생은 열여덟 살이에요.
   I am twenty years old, and my sister is eighteen years old.

제니는 예뻐요. 그리고 똑똑해요.　　Jenny is pretty. And she's smart.

→ 제니는 예쁘고 똑똑해요.　　Jenny is pretty and smart.

2) It's used when each clause are happening in sequence: and then

서점에서 책을 샀어요. 그리고 산책을 했어요.
I bought a book at the bookstore. And then I took a walk.

→ 서점에서 책을 사고[1] 산책을 했어요.
   I bought a book at the bookstore and took a walk.

한국어 공부할 거예요. 그리고 잘 거예요.
I will study Korean. And then I will go to sleep.

→ 한국어 공부하고[1] 잘 거예요. I will study Korean and then go to sleep.

✓
It is possible to connect multiple sentences with -고.

저는 스무 살이고 학생이고 미국 사람이에요.
I am twenty years old, a student, and American.

책을 읽고 청소를 하고 저녁을 먹었어요.
I read a book, cleaned, and had dinner.

✓
-고요 is used to continue or add information to something mentioned. It means 'also' or 'as well'.

제니는 노래를 잘 해요. 춤도 잘 추고요. Jenny sings well. She also dances well.

[1] Tense is applied only in the second clause, not in the first.

WORDS
간호사 [gan·ho·sa] nurse
산책하다 [san·chaek·ha·da] to take a walk
똑똑하다 [ttok·ttok·ha·da] to be smart

Master Grammar By Practicing!

🎧 09-01P.mp3

A Change the word into the form using the conjunction '-고'.

춤추다 + 그리고 → <u>춤추고</u>

1. 맵다 + 그리고 → _____
2. 학생이다 + 그리고 → _____
3. 빌리다 + 그리고 → _____
4. 초대하다 + 그리고 → _____

B Combine the two separate sentences into one sentence using '-고'.

저는 피자를 먹어요. 친구는 햄버거를 먹어요. → <u>저는 피자를 먹고 친구는 햄버거를 먹어요.</u>

1. 이 음식은 매워요. 이 음식은 짜요. → _____
2. 저는 영화를 봤어요. 제니는 탁구를 쳤어요. → _____
3. 엄마는 선생님이에요. 아빠는 경찰이에요. → _____
4. 저는 일본에 갔어요. 언니는 캐나다에 갔어요. → _____

C Look at the pictures and write a sentence that describes a sequence of actions you will do.

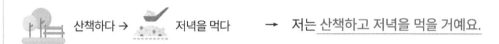

산책하다 → 저녁을 먹다 → 저는 <u>산책하고 저녁을 먹을 거예요.</u>

1. 테니스를 치다 → 집에서 쉬다 → 저는 _____
2. 공부하다 → 편의점에 가다 → 저는 _____
3. 커피를 마시다 → 신문을 읽다 → 저는 _____
4. 이메일을 보내다 → 노래를 연습하다 → 저는 _____

WORDS

피자 [pi·ja] pizza **햄버거** [haem·beo·geo] hamburger **짜다** [jja·da] to be salty
경찰 [gyeong·chal] police **캐나다** [kae·na·da] Canada **편의점** [pyeon·ui·jeom] convenience store
신문 [sin·mun] newspaper **연습하다** [yeon·seup·ha·da] to practice

UNIT 2 V-아/어서 ① (and then)

09-02G.mp3

김치를 사서 김치찌개를 만들었어요.   나는 친구를 만나서 같이 학교에 갈 거야.
I bought kimchi and made kimchi jjigae.   I will meet my friend and then go to school together.

❶ V-아/어서 [a/eo·seo] : **and then¹**

▸ -아/어서 is a connective ending to connect two clauses, showing the sequence of events.

▸ The first clause describes an action that happens before the action in the second clause.

❷ Rules²

> If the last vowel of the stem is ㅏ or ㅗ → Stem + 아서
>
> If the last vowel of the stem is neither ㅏ nor ㅗ → Stem + 어서
>
> For all of the words ending with 하다 → 하 + 여서 → 해서

영화관에 가서³ 영화를 봤어요.   I went to the theater and watched a movie.

소파에 앉아서³ 드라마를 볼 거예요. I will sit on the couch and watch a drama.

❸ Difference between -아/서 and -고

▸ Both are used to express a sequence of actions, similar to 'and then'.
However, -아/어서 is used when two actions are closely related,
while -고 connects two actions that occur sequentially but are not related.

-아/서   -고

수영을 해서 집에 갔어요. (X)   수영을 하고 집에 갔어요. (O)

I swam and then went home. (The two actions are sequential but not related.)

수영장에 가서 수영했어요. (O)   수영장에 가고 수영했어요. (X)

I went to the swimming pool and then swam.
(Going to the swimming pool is directly related to the action of swimming.)

¹ There is another use of -아/어서 for expressing causal relationship, similar to 'because'. You will learn about this in the next chapter.

² Easy way: Add 서 to the conjugated form (from which 요 is removed in the present tense).

³ Tense is applied only in the second clause, not in the first.

WORDS   영화관 [yeong·hwa·gwan] movie theater   소파 [so·pa] sofa   수영장 [su·yeong·jang] swimming pool

Master Grammar By Practicing!

PRACTICE

🎧 09-02P.mp3

A Change the word into the form using the conjunction '-아/어서'.

씻다	→	씻어서

1. 만들다 → _____
2. 일어나다 → _____
3. 듣다 → _____
4. 고르다 → _____

B Look at the pictures and write a sentence that describes a sequence of actions you will do.

친구를 만나다 → 영화를 보다 → 저는 <u>친구를 만나서 영화를 볼 거예요.</u>

1. 지하철역에 가다 → 지하철을 타다 → 저는 _____

2. 선물을 사다 → 제니한테 주다 → 저는 _____

3. 일찍 일어나다 → 운동하다 → 저는 _____

4. 사과를 씻다 → 먹다 → 저는 _____

C Choose the correct option between '-아/어서' and '-고'.

소파에 (앉아서 / 앉고) 음악을 들어요.

1. 백화점에 (가서 / 가고) 가구를 샀어요.

2. 아침 일곱 시에 아침을 (먹어서 / 먹고) 학교에 가요.

3. 주말에 친구랑 화장품을 (사서 / 사고) 스파게티를 먹을 거예요.

4. 목걸이를 (사서 / 사고) 애인에게 선물했어요.

WORDS

지하철역 [ji·ha·cheol·yeok] subway station **지하철** [ji·ha·cheol] subway   **가구** [ga·gu] furniture

화장품 [hwa·jang·pum] cosmetics   **스파게티** [seu·pa·ge·ti] spaghetti

목걸이 [mok·geo·ri] necklace   **애인** [ae·in] lover

09-03G.mp3

대학에서 공부하거나 회사에서 일할 거예요.
I will either study at the university or work at a company.

그 약은 쓰거나 실 거예요.
That medicine will be bitter or sour.

❶ A/V-거나 [geo·na] : or

▶ -거나 is a connective ending used to express a choice or alternative between two or more actions or states.[1]

❷ Rules

> Stem + 거나
>
> 가다 (to go) → 가거나   먹다 (to eat) → 먹거나
> 예쁘다 (to be pretty) → 예쁘거나   덥다 (to be hot) → 덥거나

내일 산책을 하거나 도서관에 갈 거예요.
I will either go for a walk or go to the library tomorrow.

아침에는 빵을 먹거나 그냥 우유만 마셔요.
In the morning, I either eat bread or just drink milk.

[1] -거나 is used in the cases of verbs and adjectives, while -(이)나 is used in the case of nouns. N(이)나 is taught in Chapter 9 of the Level1 book.
저는 아침이나 저녁에 운동해요.

🔥 **Useful Korean Phrase**

> V-거나 V-거나
>
> It's an expression indicating indifference between options. The content before and after -거나 typically represents contrasting or significantly different meanings.
>
> 싸거나 비싸거나 컴퓨터는 꼭 사세요.
> Whether it's cheap or expensive, make sure to buy a computer.
>
> 헨리는 시험이 있거나 없거나 열심히 공부해요.
> Henry studies hard, whether there's an exam or not.

WORDS   쓰다 [sseu·da] to be bitter   시다 [si·da] to be sour   그냥 [geu·nyang] just, simply

Master Grammar By Practicing!

♪ 09-03P.mp3

A Choose the correct option.

> 남자친구랑 커피를 (마시거나 / 마시나) 식사를 할 거예요.

1. 자전거를 (탈거나 / 타거나) 수영을 할 거예요.
2. 일찍 (자거나 / 자나) 계속 공부할 거예요.
3. 그림을 (그리거나 / 그리나) 사진을 찍어요.
4. 주말에 여행을 (할거나 / 하거나) 집에서 쉴 거예요.

B Combine the two separate sentences into one sentence using '-거나'.

> 한국 음식은 매워요. (한국 음식은) 짜요. → <u>한국 음식은 맵거나 짜요.</u>

1. 주말에 외국어를 배워요. (주말에) 축구를 해요. → _____
2. 파티에서 노래를 부를 거예요. (파티에서) 춤을 출 거예요. → _____
3. 약국에서 감기약을 살 거예요. 병원에 갈 거예요. → _____
4. 일요일에 청소를 할 거예요. (일요일에) 빨래를 할 거예요. → _____

C Rewrite the sentence using 'noun + (이)나' format.

> 콜라를 마시거나 주스를 마셔요 → <u>콜라나 주스를 마셔요.</u>

1. 주말에 영화를 보거나 연극을 볼 거예요. → 주말에 _____ 볼 거예요.
2. 저는 매일 테니스를 치거나 탁구를 쳐요. → 저는 매일 _____ 쳐요.
3. 벽에 시계를 걸거나 달력을 걸고 싶어요. → 벽에 _____ 걸고 싶어요.
4. 저희는 1월에 고향에 가거나 2월에 고향에 가요. → 저희는 _____ 고향에 가요.

WORDS

계속 [gye·sok] continuously
약국 [yak·guk] pharmacy
연극 [yeon·geuk] play (theater)

감기 [gam·gi] cold (illness)
빨래하다 [ppal·lae·ha·da] to do laundry
시계 [si·gye] watch, clock   달력 [dal·lyeok] calendar

UNIT 4 | A/V-지만 (but, however)

🎧 09-04G.mp3

제니는 미국 사람이지만 한국어를 참 잘해요.
Jenny is American, but she speaks Korean very well.

우체국에 갔지만 제 소포가 거기 없었어요.
I went to the post office, but my parcel wasn't there.

① A/V-지만 [ju·man] : but

▶ -지만 is a connective ending used to express contrast between two clauses, similar to 'but' or 'however' in English.

② Rules

> **Stem + 지만**
>
> 가다 (to go) → 가지만 　　　　먹다 (to eat) → 먹지마
> 예쁘다 (to be pretty) → 예쁘지만 　　덥다 (to be hot) → 덥지만
>
> In the case of past tense, -지만 is added to -았/었.
>
> 가다 (to go) → 갔지만 　　　　먹다 (to eat) → 먹었지만
> 예쁘다 (to be pretty) → 예뻤지만 　　덥다 (to be hot) → 더웠지만

[1] 배가 고프다 literally means "My stomach is hungry". The opposite expression, 배가 부르다, translates to "My stomach is full", which simply means "I am full".

배가 고파요.[1] 하지만 조금만 먹을 거예요.　　I'm hungry. But I will eat just a little.

배가 고프지만 조금만 먹을 거예요.　　I'm hungry, but I will eat just a little.

저는 어제 일을 많이 했어요. 하지만 피곤하지 않아요.
I worked a lot yesterday. But I am not tired.

저는 어제 일을 많이 했지만[2] 피곤하지 않아요.
I worked a lot yesterday, but I am not tired.)

[2] Maintaining the tense of the first clause, it is written as 일을 많이 했지만.

WORDS　　우체국 [u·che·guk] post office　　　　참 [cham] really, truly
　　　　　　피곤하다 [pi·gon·ha·da] to be tired

Master Grammar By Practicing!

🎧 09-04P.mp3

A Convert the word into the form using the conjunction '-지만'.

깨끗하다 + 하지만	→	깨끗하지만

1. 신다 + 하지만 → _____
2. 찍다 + 하지만 → _____
3. 재미없다 + 하지만 → _____
4. 짜다 + 하지만 → _____

B Choose the option that matches the tense.

> 저는 영화를 (좋아하지만 / 좋아했지만) 드라마는 별로 안 좋아해요.

1. 영화를 (보려고 하지만 / 보려고 했지만) 시간이 없었어요.
2. 어제 너무 (바쁘지만 / 바빴지만) 여자친구를 만났어요.
3. 그 드라마는 (재미있지만 / 재미있었지만) 너무 길어요.
4. 저는 작년에 대학교를 (졸업하지만 / 졸업했지만) 일하지 않아요.

C Combine the two separate sentences into one sentence using '-지만'.

이 공원은 아름다워요. 사람이 많아요.	→	이 공원은 아름답지만 사람이 많아요.

1. 한국 음식을 좋아해요. 아직 젓가락을 못 써요. → _____
2. 저는 요리를 자주 해요. 제 음식은 맛없어요. → _____
3. 배가 아팠어요. 병원에 가지 않았어요. → _____
4. 공항에 갔어요. 친구를 못 만났어요. → _____

WORDS

별로 [byeol·lo] not much, not really   **대학교** [dae·hak·gyo] university   **아직** [a·jik] still, yet
젓가락 [jeot·ga·rak] chopsticks   **맛없다** [mat·eop·tta] to taste bad, to not be delicious
배 [bae] stomach   **공항** [gong·hang] airport

🎧 09-05G.mp3

제 남자친구는 멋있는데 조금 재미없어요.
My boyfriend is cool, but he's a little boring.

지금 봄인데 아직 추워요.
It's spring now, but it's still cold.end.

❶ V/A-(으)ㄴ/는데 [(eun)/neun·de] : **but**

▶ -(으)ㄴ/는데 are connective endings used when the first clause provides contrast in relation to the second clause.

❷ Rules

If the word is a **verb** → Verb stem + 는데
먹다(to eat) → 먹는데   가다(to go) → 가는데

If the word is an **adjective,**[1]
and it ends in a consonant → Adjective stem + 은데
삭나(to be small) → 삭 + 은데 → 작은데

and it ends in a vowel → Adjective stem + ㄴ데
크다(to be big) → 크 + ㄴ데 → 큰데

If the word is a 이다 → 이다 + ㄴ데 → 인데
학생이다 (to be a student) → 학생인데

엄마는 키가 커요. 그런데 저는 키가 작아요.   My mom is tall. But I am short.
엄마는 키가 큰데 저는 키가 작아요.   My mom is tall, but I am short.

밥을 많이 먹었어요. 그런데 배가 안 불러요.   I ate a lot. But I'm not full.
밥을 많이 먹었는데 배가 안 불러요.   I ate a lot, but I'm not full.

❸ Differences between -지만 and -(으)ㄴ/는데

▶ Both -지만 and -(으)ㄴ/는데 are used to connect contrasting clauses, so they can be interchanged, but there is a slight nuance difference.

▶ When -지만 is replaced with -(으)ㄴ/는데, the meaning of 'but' becomes somewhat softer.

▶ -(으)ㄴ/는데 is used more often than 지만 in everyday spoken conversation.

✓
If it's the past tense
→ -았/었 + 는데
먹다 → 먹었는데
작다 → 작았는데
크다 → 컸는데
이다 → 였는데

[1] If an adjective ends with 있다 or 없다, 는데 is attached instead of 은데.
맛있다 → 맛있는데
맛있은데 (X)
맛없다 → 맛없는데
맛없은데 (X)

✓
For ㅂ irregular adjectives, the ㅂ is dropped and replaced with 우.

춥다: 춥 → 추우 + ㄴ데
→ 추운데, 춥은데 (X)

맵다: 맵 → 매우 + ㄴ데
→ 매운데, 맵은데 (X)

Master Grammar By Practicing!

🎧 09-05P.mp3

A Choose the correct option.

> 저는 운동을 (좋아하는데 / 좋아한는데) 시간이 없어요.

1. 오늘 (주말이는데 / 주말인데) 날씨가 안 좋아요.

2. 새 영화를 (봤는데 / 봤은데) 지루했어요.

3. 식당에 사람이 (많은데 / 많는데) 조용해요.

4. 한국 음식은 (맵운데 / 매운데) 맛있어요.

B Correct the underlined part, in case it is incorrect.

> 저는 책을 자주 읽은데 이번 주에는 한 권밖에 못 읽었어요. (correct / incorrect) → 읽는데

1. 이 케이크는 맛있은데 너무 달아요. (correct / incorrect) → _____

2. 오빠는 키가 크은데 농구를 잘 못해요. (correct / incorrect) → _____

3. 저 식당은 유명한데 맛이 별로 없어요. (correct / incorrect) → _____

4. 요즘 겨울이는데 냉면을 먹었어요. (correct / incorrect) → _____

C Combine the two separate sentences into one sentence using '-(으)ㄴ/는데'.

> 노래를 잘 못 불렀어요. 기분이 좋았어요. → 노래를 잘 못 불렀는데 기분이 좋았어요.

1. 점심을 많이 먹었어요. 배가 고파요. → _____

2. 화요일마다 피아노를 배워요. 피아노를 잘 못 쳐요. → _____

3. 이 물건은 가격이 비싸요. 별로 안 좋아요. → _____

4. 저는 인도네시아 사람이에요. 한국어를 잘해요. → _____

WORDS

새 [sae] new   **지루하다** [ji·ru·ha·da] to be boring   **조용하다** [jo·yong·ha·da] to be quiet
농구 [nong·gu] basketball   **유명하다** [yu·myeong·ha·da] to be famous
냉면 [naeng·myeon] cold noodles   **기분** [gi·bun] mood
가격 [ga·gyeok] price   **인도네시아** [in·do·ne·si·a] Indonesia

🎧 09-C.mp3

요코: 민호 씨, 미국 잘 다녀왔어요? Did you have a good trip to the US?

민호: 네, 잘 다녀왔어요. 정말 재미있었어요. Yes, I had a great time. It was really fun.

요코: 어느 도시에 갔어요? Which cities did you go to?

민호: 라스베가스에도 가고 샌프란시스코에도 갔어요.
I went to Las Vegas and also to San Francisco.

요코: 라스베가스에 가서 뭐 했어요? What did you do in Las Vegas?

민호: 콘서트도 보고 호텔도 구경했어요. I saw a concert and looked around the hotels.

호텔이 정말 크고 좋았는데 아주 쌌어요.
The hotels were really big and nice, but very cheap.

요코: 영어는 어땠어요? How was your English?

민호: 잘 하지 못했지만 괜찮았어요. I didn't do well, but it was okay.

구글이 영어를 잘 했어요. Google was good at English.

✏️ 다녀오다 combines 다니다 (to go around/attend) and 오다 (to come). It literally means 'go and come', but the term is used to describe leaving for a place and then returning from it, often implying a successful or satisfactory visit.

✏️ When listing items that share the same predicate, the particle 도 is used, resulting in the form -도 A/V고 -도 A/V.
라스베가스에 갔어요. 그리고 샌프란시스코에 갔어요. → 라스베가스에도 가고 샌프란시스코에도 갔어요.
사과를 좋아해요. 바나나를 좋아해요. → 사과도 좋아하고 바나나도 좋아해요.

RECAP CHAPTER 9

❶ A/V-고: and, and then

1) Used to list of actions or states: and
2) Used when each clause are happening in sequence: and then

When linking two sentences with 그리고 → stem + 고

❷ V-아/어서: and then

Used to connect two clauses, showing the sequence of events, especially when the two actions are closely related

If the last vowel of the stem is ㅏ or ㅗ → stem + 아서
If the last vowel of the stem is neither ㅏ nor ㅗ → stem + 어서
Every verbs with 하다 → 하다 changes to 해서

❸ A/V-거나: or

Used to express a choice or alternative between two or more actions or states
stem + 거나

❹ A/V-지만: but, however

Used to express contrast between two clauses

When linking two sentences with 하지만 → stem + 지만

❺ A/V-(으)ㄴ/는데: but

Used to express contrast between two clauses
Used more frequently than 지만 in everyday conversations.

If the word is a verb → stem + 는데
If the word is an adjective, and it ends in a consonant → stem + 은데
If the word is an adjective, and it ends in a vowel → stem + ㄴ데
If the word is a 이다 → stem + ㄴ데 → 인데

REVIEW TEST CHAPTER 9

A Choose the option that is paired with the correct answers.

> 옷을 (   ) 밖으로 나갔어요.
> 포도를 (   ) 친구랑 같이 먹었어요.

① 입고 - 씻고   ② 입어서 - 씻고

③ 입고 - 씻어서   ④ 입어서 - 씻어서

B Choose the sentence where the underlined word is **incorrect**.

① 저 사람은 <u>선생님이거나</u> 의사예요.

② 영화를 <u>볼거나</u> 운동을 할 거예요.

③ 아침에 공원에서 <u>달리거나</u> 수영을 해요.

④ 선생님께 <u>물어보거나</u> 이메일을 보내세요.

C Choose the correct option of the underlined verb in the '-(으)ㄴ/는데' form.

> 떡볶이는 <u>맛있다</u> 너무 매워요.
> 가방이 <u>예쁘다</u> 너무 비싸요.

① 맛있는데 - 예쁜데   ② 맛있는데 - 예쁘는데

③ 맛있는데 - 예쁘는데   ④ 맛있은데 - 예쁜데

D In the following passage, choose the option that is written **incorrectly**.

> 제니는 미국으로 돌아갔어요. 지난 3월에 대학교를 ①졸업하고 제니의 부모님 댁으로 이사했어요. 제니는 미국에 ②갔어서 일을 찾았어요. 저는 제니한테 ③전화하거나 이메일을 써요. 우리 모두 ④바쁘지만 자주 연락하고 있어요.

E Choose the **incorrect** sentence.

① 테니스를 치고 집에 갔어요.

② 옷을 벗어서 벽에 걸었어요.

③ 열심히 공부하지만 시험을 못 봤어요.

④ 춤을 추거나 노래를 부를 거예요.

F Choose the word that commonly fits into the two blank spaces.

> 이 사탕은 달____ 조금 셔요.
> 저는 여행을 좋아하____ 돈이 없어요.

① 아서   ② 지만

③ 은데   ④ 고

G Read the following dialogue and choose the **incorrect** statement.

> 유코: 헨리 씨는 취미가 뭐예요?
> 헨리: 저는 등산 좋아해요.
>   일요일마다 아침을 먹고 산에 가요.
>   산에 올라가서 사진도 많이 찍어요.
> 유코: 산이 집에서 가까워요?
>   저도 등산 좋아하는데 산이 없어요.
> 헨리: 네, 아주 가깝지 않지만 멀지도 않아요.
> 유코: 저도 산이 가까웠으면 좋겠어요.

① 헨리의 취미는 등산입니다.

② 헨리는 일요일 아침에 등산을 합니다.

③ 헨리는 산에서 아침을 먹습니다.

④ 유코의 집은 산에서 멉니다.

🎧 09-V.mp3

No.	✓	Word	Meaning	No.	✓	Word	Meaning
1	☐	아직		26	☐	똑똑하다	
2	☐	지루하다		27	☐	피자	
3	☐	햄버거		28	☐	젓가락	
4	☐	지하철		29	☐	별로	
5	☐	지하철역		30	☐	조용하다	
6	☐	배 (body)		31	☐	산책하다	
7	☐	가격		32	☐	그냥	
8	☐	애인		33	☐	연습하다	
9	☐	참		34	☐	기분	
10	☐	유명하다		35	☐	대학교	
11	☐	농구		36	☐	신문	
12	☐	새		37	☐	캐나다	
13	☐	시다		38	☐	목걸이	
14	☐	영화관		39	☐	수영장	
15	☐	맛없다		40	☐	편의점	
16	☐	시계		41	☐	공항	
17	☐	간호사		42	☐	소파	
18	☐	달력		43	☐	연극	
19	☐	짜다		44	☐	인도네시아	
20	☐	피곤하다		45	☐	빨래하다	
21	☐	약국		46	☐	가구	
22	☐	계속		47	☐	화장품	
23	☐	쓰다		48	☐	경찰	
24	☐	우체국		49	☐	감기	
25	☐	스파게티		50	☐	냉면	

Number of words I've learned: _____ / 50

Korean Traditional Clothing 'Hanbok'

Hanbok is a traditional Korean costume that creates elegance through the harmony of straight lines and curves. Although the basic color is white, as implied by the term "Baekui minjok" (the white-clad ethnic group), the way it is worn, materials, and colors vary depending on the season and social status. Shall we explore how Hanbok is composed?

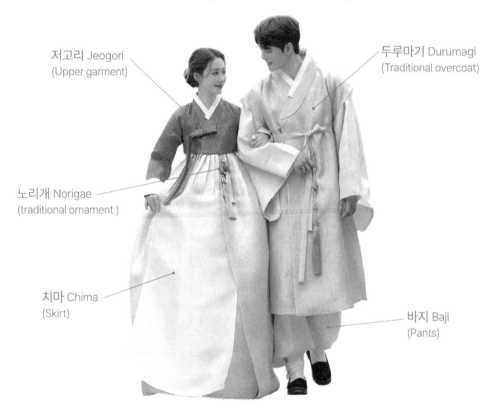

저고리 Jeogori
(Upper garment)

두루마기 Durumagi
(Traditional overcoat)

노리개 Norigae
(traditional ornament)

치마 Chima
(Skirt)

바지 Baji
(Pants)

Hanbok is a beautiful attire that represents the culture and tradition of South Korea, often worn on special occasions and events. Recently, the design and style of Hanbok have undergone modern transformations, resulting in a variety of colorful Hanbok options that cater to different tastes and preferences.

Since 2013, there has been free admission to Gyeongbokgung Palace in Seoul if you come wearing a Hanbok. You can rent a Hanbok from rental shops nearby. Why not try strolling through Gyeongbokgung Palace in a Hanbok during your visit to Korea?

CHAPTER 10
Connecting Sentences: Causes and Reasons

🔘 What you'll learn in this chapter

Chapter 10 is dedicated to expressing causes and reasons, a fundamental component of effective communication. You'll learn how to construct sentences that explain motives, reasons, and causes, using various structures that correspond to phrases like 'because', 'since', and 'due to' in English. By the end of this chapter, you will be better equipped to clearly express the reasons behind actions and opinions.

🎧 10-01G.mp3

일을 많이 해서 피곤해요.
I'm tired because I worked a lot.

배가 고파서 점심을 일찍 먹었어요.
I had lunch early because I was hungry.

❶ V-아/어서 [a/eo·seo] : because, so

▶ -아/어서 is a connective ending used to express reason or cause, similar to 'because' or 'so' in English.

▶ The information in the first clause represents the reason or cause of the action described in the second clause.

[1] Easy way: Add 서 to the conjugated form (from which 요 is removed in the present tense).

❷ Rules[1]

> If the last vowel of the stem is ㅏ or ㅗ → Stem + 아서
>
> If the last vowel of the stem is neither ㅏ nor ㅗ → Stem + 어서
>
> For all of the words ending with 하다 → 하 + 여서 → 해서

[2] Tense is applied only in the second clause, not in the first. 비가 왔어서 밖에 안 나갔어요. (X)

비가 왔어요. 그래서 밖에 안 나갔어요. It was raining, so I didn't go outside.

비가 와서[2] 밖에 안 나갔어요. I didn't go outside because it was raining.

밥을 많이 먹어서 배가 불러요. I'm full because I ate a lot.

오늘 너무 피곤해서 집에서 쉬었어요. I rested at home today because I was so tired.

이다 (to be) → 이 + 어서 → 이어서[3]

친구이다: 친구 + 이어서 → 친구이어서 (shortened to: 친구여서)

학생이다: 학생 + 이어서 → 학생이어서

아니다 (to not be) → 아니 + 어서 → 아니어서

친구가 아니어서, 학생이 아니어서

[3] -(이)라서 is the same as -이어서 and is used more often than the -이어서 form in everyday conversations.

학생 + 이라서 → 학생이라서
친구 + 라서 → 친구라서
우리는 <u>친구라서</u> 자주 만나요.
=우리는 <u>친구여서</u> 자주 만나요.
We often meet because we are friends.

⚠ In sentences with -아/어서, request and command sentences cannot follow in the second clause.[4]

시간이 없어서 택시를 탈까요? (X) We don't have time, so shall we take a taxi?

제 친구가 <u>와서</u> 조금만 기다리세요. (X) My friend is coming, so wait a moment.

[4] You will learn how to express reasons in request and command sentences in the next unit.

Master Grammar By Practicing!

 10-01P.mp3

A Change the given word to complete the sentence using '-아/어서'.

있다 (to have)	→	내일 시험이 <u>있어서</u> 공부를 열심히 했어요.

1. 재미있다 (to be interesting) → 영화가 _____ 두 번이나 봤어요.

2. 거짓말하다 (to lie) → 친구가 _____ 화가 났어요.

3. 걷다 (to walk) → 너무 오래 _____ 발가락이 아파요.

4. 어렵다 (to be difficult) → 한국어가 _____ 학원에 다니기로 했어요.

B Combine the two separate sentences into one sentence, using '-아/어서'.

강아지가 불쌍해요. 밥을 줬어요.	→	<u>강아지가 불쌍해서 밥을 줬어요.</u>

1. 길을 몰라요. 지도를 봤어요. → _____

2. 요즘 외로워요. 남자친구를 사귀고 싶어요. → _____

3. 내일이 친구 생일이에요. 파티를 할 거예요. → _____

4. 비가 왔어요. 우산을 샀어요. → _____

C Choose the appropriate word and complete the question, using '-아/어서'.

싸우다	보다	많다	지루하다	잃어버리다

A: 수업에 왜 늦었어요?	B: 시간을 잘못 <u>봐서</u> 늦었어요.

1. A: 남자친구랑 왜 말 안 해요? B: 남자친구랑 _____ 안 해요.

2. A: 전화 왜 안 받아? B: 핸드폰을 _____ 못 받았어.

3. A: 어제 일찍 잤어요? B: 아니요, 일이 _____ 일찍 못 잤어요.

4. A: 그 드라마 어땠어요? B: 너무 _____ 다 안 봤어요.

WORDS

화 [hwa] anger   화나다 [hwa·na·da] to be angry   발가락 [bal·ga·rak] toe

불쌍하다 [bul·ssang·ha·da] to be pitiful, to feel sorry for   지도 [ji·do] map

외롭다 [oe·rop·tta] to be lonely   잘못 [jal·mot] mistake, wrong; by mistake, wrongly

싸우다 [ssa·u·da] to fight   잃어버리다 [i·reo·beo·ri·da] to lose (something)

UNIT 2 | A/V-(으)니까 ① (because)

🎧 10-02G.mp3

배가 고프니까 저녁을 준비할게요.
Since I'm hungry, I will prepare dinner.

비가 오니까 우산을 가져가세요.
Since it's raining, please take an umbrella.

❶ A/V-(으)니까¹ [(eu)·ni·kka] : because, since

▶ -(으)니까 is used to express a cause or reason. It indicates the reason for an action or situation that is mentioned in the following clause.

많이 잤어요. 그러니까 안 피곤할 거예요. I slept a lot, so I won't be tired.
많이 잤으니까² 안 피곤할 거예요. Since I slept a lot, I won't be tired.

손가락이 다쳤으니까 병원에 가세요.³ Your finger is hurt, so go to the hospital.

❷ Differences between -아/어서 and -(으)니까

A/V-아/어서	A/V-(으)니까
It cannot be used in request and command sentences	It can be used in request and command sentences
배고파서 식당에 갑시다. (X)	배고프니까 식당에 갑시다. (O) Let's go to the restaurant since I'm hungry.
It cannot combine with the past tense.	It can combine with the past tense.
물이 뜨거웠어서 마시지 못했어요. (X) 물이 뜨거워서 마시지 못했어요. (O)	물이 뜨거웠으니까 마시지 못했어요. (O) I couldn't drink the water since it was too hot.
It's used mainly to express a general reason.	It's used to express the subjective reason.
겨울이 와서 날씨가 추워요. It's cold because winter has come.	민수는 안 친절하니까 친구가 없어요. Minsu has no friends because he's not kind.
It's used to express the reason for one's emotions, often appearing in greetings.	It is not used in greetings, nor is it used in sentences expressing emotions.
시험을 잘 봐서 기뻐요. (O) I'm happy because I did well on the exam. 만나서 반가워요. (O) Nice to meet you.	시험을 잘 보니까 너무 기뻐요. (X) 만나니까 반가워요. (X) 도와주시니까 감사합니다. (X)

¹ If the stem ends in a consonant
→ stem + 으니까
먹다 → 먹으니까
If the stem ends in a vowel or ㄹ → stem + 니까
자다 → 자니까
만들다 → 만드니까

² In a -니까 clause, you can use past or future tense.
= 많이 자서 안 피곤할 거예요.

³ In sentences with -(으)니까, request and command sentences can follow in the second clause.

WORDS

손가락 [son·ga·rak] finger **다치다** [da·chi·da] to be hurt **그러니까** [geu·reo·ni·kka] so, therefore
친절하다 [chin·jeol·ha·da] to be kind **기쁘다** [gi·ppeu·da] to be glad

Master Grammar By Practicing!

A Change the given word to complete the sentence, using '-(으)니까'.

🎧 10-02P.mp3

배고프다 (to be hungry)	→ 배고프니까 저 식당에 가서 식사할까요?

1. 더럽다 (to be dirty) → 이 호텔은 _____ 다른 호텔로 갈까요?

2. 시험 보다 (to take a exam) → 내일 _____ 너무 늦게 자지 마.

3. 맛있다 (to be delicious) → 이 샌드위치가 _____ 이거 드세요.

4. 시간이 없다 (to not have time) → _____ 회의는 다음 주에 합시다.

B Combine the two separate sentences into one sentence, using '-(으)니까'.

잠을 못 잤어요. 집에서 쉴래요.	→ 잠을 못 잤으니까 집에서 쉴래요.

1. 손님이 와요. 청소를 해요. → _____

2. 얼음이 진짜 차가워요. 조심하세요. → _____

3. 방이 어두워요. 불을 켜 주세요. → _____

4. 그 영화 무서워요. 놀라지 마세요. → _____

C Choose the correct option between '-아/어서' and '-(으)니까'.

함께 (일할 수 있으니까 / 일할 수 있어서) 기뻐요.

1. 여기가 좀 (시끄러우니까 / 시끄러워서) 저쪽으로 갈까요?

2. 국이 (뜨거워서 / 뜨거우니까) 천천히 드세요.

3. 이사 (도와주셔서 / 도와주시니까) 감사합니다.

4. (늦어서 / 늦었으니까) 죄송해요.

WORDS

더럽다 [deo·reop·tta] to be dirty   **샌드위치** [saen·deu·wi·chi] sandwich   **얼음** [eo·reum] ice

차갑다 [cha·gap·tta] to be cold   **어둡다** [eo·dup·tta] to be dark

무섭다 [mu·seop·tta] to be scary   **놀라다** [nol·la·da] to be surprised

시끄럽다 [si·kkeu·reop·tta] to be noisy   **뜨겁다** [tteu·geop·tta] to be hot

🎧 10-03G.mp3

눈 때문에 약속을 취소했어요
I canceled the plan because of the snow.

회사가 멀기 때문에 집에서 일찍 나가요.
I leave home early because the company is far away.

❶ N 때문에 [ttae·mu·ne]: **because of N, due to N**

▶ 때문에 is used to express the cause or reason for something.

▶ It is attached to a noun, regardless of whether the noun is a consonant or a vowel.

모기 때문에 잠을 하나도 못 잤어요.
I couldn't sleep at all because of mosquitoes.

감기 때문에 학교에 못 갔어요.
I couldn't go to school because of a cold.

❷ A/V-기¹ 때문에 [gi ttae·mu·ne]: **because**

▶ -기 때문에 is used to express the reason of the situation described in the second clause.

▶ It expresses a clearer reason compared to -아/어서 or -(으)니까.

▶ -기 때문에² is attached to a word stem, regardless of whether the stem ends in a consonant or a vowel.

먹다 (to eat) → 먹 + 기 때문에 → 먹기 때문에
오다 (to come) → 오 + 기 때문에 → 오기 때문에

비가 오기 때문에 우산을 가져갔어요.
I took an umbrella because it's raining.

한국 음식을 자주 요리하기 때문에 간장이 필요해요.
I need soy source because I often cook Korean food.

¹-기 is used to turn verbs into nouns. You will learn about its usage in Level 3.

²-기 때문에 can be combined with the past tense and is written in the form of -았/었기 때문에

커피를 많이 마셨기 때문에 잠이 안 와요. I can't sleep because I drank too much coffee.

✓
Like -아/어서, request and command sentences cannot follow in the second clause.

국이 뜨겁기 때문에 조금만 기다리세요. (X)
→ 국이 뜨거우니까 조금만 기다리세요. (O)
The soup is hot, so wait a moment.

WORDS

눈 [nun] snow
간장 [gan·jang] soy sauce

취소하다 [chwi·so·ha·da] to cancel
필요하다 [pi·ryo·ha·da] to be necessary

모기 [mo·gi] mosquito

Master Grammar By Practicing!

 10-03P.mp3

A Change the given word to complete the sentence, using '-기 때문에'.

운동하다 (to exercise)	→	저는 매일 <u>운동하기 때문에</u> 건강해요.

1. 재미있다 (to be fun) → 제니는 예쁘고 _____ 인기가 많아요.

2. 태어나다 (to be born) → 아기가 _____ 아기 방이 필요해요.

3. 젊다 (to be young) → 민호는 아직 _____ 공부를 더 하고 싶어해요.

4. 키우다 (to raise) → 강아지를 _____ 동물 병원에 자주 가요.

B Choose the appropriate word and complete the question, using '-기 때문에'.

되고 싶다　　　좋아하다　　　한국 사람이다　　　싸다　　　살다

A: 일을 왜 많이 해요?	B: 부자가 <u>되고 싶기 때문에</u> 일을 많이 해요.

1. A: 왜 시장에 가요? 　　B: 시장이 _____ 저는 시장에서 물건을 사요.

2. A: 영어를 어떻게 공부해요? 　　B: 외국에 _____ 영어를 더 자주 쓸 수 있어요.

3. A: 주말에 주로 뭘 해요? 　　B: 책을 _____ 서점에 자주 가요.

4. A: 왜 한국어를 배워요? 　　B: 남편이 _____ 한국어를 잘 하고 싶어요.

C Choose the correct option.

방이 (덥기 때문에 / 더우니까) 문 좀 열어 주세요.

1. (날씨 때문에 / 날씨어서) 여행을 취소했어요.

2. 단어를 매일 (외웠기 때문에 / 외웠어서) 한국어를 잘해요.

3. 일이 (많기 때문에 / 많으니까) 내일 일찍 출근하세요.

4. (아르바이트니까 / 아르바이트 때문에) 시간이 별로 없어요.

WORDS

인기 [in·kki] popularity　　　　태어나다 [tae·eo·na·da] to be born

젊다 [jeolm·tta] to be young　　키우다 [ki·u·da] to raise, to grow　　동물 [dong·mul] animal

부자 [bu·ja] rich person　　　　외국 [oe·guk] foreign country

외우다 [oe·u·da] to memorize　　출근하다 [chul·geun·ha·da] to go to work

🎧 10-C.mp3

마리아: 헨리 씨 어제 수업에 왜 안 왔어요?

Henry, why didn't you come to class yesterday?

헨리: 몸이 안 좋아서 집에서 쉬었어요. I wasn't feeling well, so I rested at home.

마리아: 아, 진짜요? 이제 괜찮아요? Ah, really? Are you okay now?

헨리: 네, 약 먹어서 지금은 나았어요. Yes, I took medicine, so I am better now.

마리아: 다시 아플 수 있으니까 약을 더 먹어요.

You can get sick again, so take more medicine.

헨리: 그런데 약 때문에 너무 피곤해요. But because of the medicine, I'm too tired.

그냥 약 안 먹고 더 쉴래요. I'd rather not take it and just rest more.

마리아: 네, 빨리 나으세요. Yes, get well soon.

헨리: 걱정해줘서 고마워요. Thank you for worrying about me.

✏️ The expression 몸이 안 좋다 literally means "My body is not good.", but it indicates that someone is feeling unwell or sick.

WORDS

낫다 [nat·tta] to get well   다시 [da·si] again

RECAP CHAPTER 10

❶ A/V-아/어서: because

Used to express reason or cause, when linking two sentences with 그래서

If the last vowel of the stem is ㅏ or ㅗ → stem + 아서
If the last vowel of the stem is neither ㅏ nor ㅗ → stem + 어서
Every verbs with 하다 → 하다 changes to 해서

❷ A/V-(으)니까: because

Used to express reason or cause, when linking two sentences with 그러니까

If the verb stem ends in a consonant → stem + 으니까
If the verb stem ends in a vowel → stem + 니까

❸ N 때문에: because of N, A/V-기 때문에: because

Noun + 때문에
Stem + 기 때문에

-아/어서	-(으)니까	-기 때문에
Cannot be used in request and command sentences	Can be used in request and command sentences	Cannot be used in request and command sentences
배고파서 밥을 먹읍시다. (X)	배고프니까 밥을 먹읍시다. (O)	배고프기 때문에 밥을 먹읍시다.(X)
Cannot combine with the past tense	Can combine with the past tense	Can combine with the past tense
비가 왔어서 여행 안 갔어요. (X) → 비가 와서 여행 안 갔어요. (O)	비가 왔으니까 여행 안 갔어요.(O)	비가 왔기 때문에 여행 안 갔어요. (O)
Can be used to express the reasons for emotions or in greetings	Cannot be used to express the reasons for emotions or in greetings	Cannot be used to express the reasons for emotions or in greetings
만나서 반가워요. (O)	만나니까 반가워요. (X)	만나기 때문에 반가워요. (X)

REVIEW TEST CHAPTER 10

A Choose the option that is paired with the correct answers.

> 머리가 (   ) 약을 샀어요.
>
> 담배를 (   ) 목이 아파요.

① 아파서 - 피워서　　② 아퍼서 - 피어서

③ 아퍼서 - 피워서　　④ 아파서 - 피어서

B Choose the sentence where the underlined word is correct.

① 눈이 <u>오기 때문에</u> 운전 조심하세요.

② <u>만나기 때문에</u> 반가워요.

③ 일을 많이 <u>했기 때문에</u> 조금 피곤해요.

④ 꽃이 <u>예쁘기 때문에</u> 소풍 갈까요?

C Choose the correct arrangement of the words in brackets.

> My friend went to the store because he/she wanted to buy shoes.
>
> (신발을, 제 친구는, 갔어요, 가게에, 사고 싶어서)

① 가게에 제 친구는 신발을 갔어요 사고 싶어서.

② 제 친구는 신발을 사고 싶어서 가게에 갔어요.

③ 신발을 가게에 사고 싶어서 제 친구는 갔어요.

④ 제 친구는 사고 싶어서 신발을 가게에 갔어요.

D In the following passage, choose the option that is written **incorrectly**.

> 요즘 날씨가 ①좋아서 밖에 자주 나가요. 오늘은 시간이 ②있었기 때문에 친구를 만났어요. 오랜만에 친구를 ③만나서 반가웠어요. 이야기를 너무 많이 ④하기 때문에 목이 아팠어요.

E Choose the **incorrect** sentence.

① 날씨가 흐려서 우산을 가져갔어요.

② 저를 도와주니까 고마워요.

③ 너무 늦었으니까 집에 갑시다.

④ 친구가 놀러 와서 기분 좋아요.

F Choose the sentence that does **not** make sense.

① 다리를 다쳐서 병원에 갔어요.

② 음식이 너무 짜서 물을 넣었어요.

③ 너무 슬퍼서 울었어요.

④ 케이크가 써서 맛있었어요.

G Read the following phone call and choose the **incorrect** statement.

> 민호: 지수야, 지금 뭐해?
>
> 지수: 나 지금 심심해서 드라마 보고 있어.
>
> 민호: 그럼 우리 지금 만날래?
>
> 지수: 좋아. 어디에서 만날까?
>
> 민호: 식당에서 만나자.
>
> 　　　배고프니까 저녁 같이 먹자.
>
> 지수: 나 지금 다이어트 때문에 저녁 안 먹어.
>
> 　　　그냥 커피나 마시자.

① 지수는 심심해서 드라마를 봅니다.

② 민호는 지수를 만나고 싶습니다.

③ 민호와 지수는 식당에서 저녁을 먹습니다.

④ 지수는 다이어트를 하고 있습니다.

🎧 10-V.mp3

No.	✓	Word	Meaning
1	☐	기쁘다	
2	☐	동물	
3	☐	다시	
4	☐	태어나다	
5	☐	싸우다	
6	☐	눈	
7	☐	화	
8	☐	차갑다	
9	☐	손가락	
10	☐	뜨겁다	
11	☐	어둡다	
12	☐	놀라다	
13	☐	다치다	
14	☐	낫다	
15	☐	취소하다	
16	☐	모기	
17	☐	불쌍하다	
18	☐	그러니까	
19	☐	샌드위치	
20	☐	외롭다	
21	☐	무섭다	
22	☐	더럽다	
23	☐	화나다	
24	☐	필요하다	
25	☐	외국	

No.	✓	Word	Meaning
26	☐	지도	
27	☐	시끄럽다	
28	☐	부자	
29	☐	인기	
30	☐	잃어버리다	
31	☐	얼음	
32	☐	출근하다	
33	☐	키우다	
34	☐	외우다	
35	☐	친절하다	
36	☐	잘못	
37	☐	간장	
38	☐	발가락	
39	☐	젊다	

Number of words I've learned: _____ / 39

Exploring Korean Superstitions: Taboos in daily life

In Korea, a range of taboos and symbols of ill fortune rooted in superstition and tradition has been observed since ancient times. Let's delve into some representative examples:

Placing spoons or chopsticks vertically in rice

In daily life, Koreans avoid placing spoons or chopsticks vertically in rice, as this behavior is reserved for 제사 (Jesa) - a ritual where food is offered to ancestors during memorial services. Performing this action unconsciously is considered very rude and disrespectful and should be avoided.

Writing names in red ink

There exists a superstition in Korea that writing someone's name in red ink can bring misfortune to that person. This belief is thought to have originated during the Korean War, when the names of deceased soldiers were marked in red on notification letters, causing great sorrow among families. Consequently, writing a living person's name in red is now considered a taboo.

Eating seaweed soup before an exam

It is also taboo to eat seaweed soup before an exam. The slippery and slimy nature of seaweed leads to the belief that one might "slip" during the exam, symbolically. To counter this, there is a tradition of eating sticky foods like taffy or sticky rice cakes before exams, symbolizing a desire for success.

The number 4

In many East Asian cultures, including Korea, the number 4 is considered unlucky because it sounds similar to the word for 'death' in Chinese characters. It is common practice to see the 4th floor labeled as 'F' or even omitted entirely in many Korean buildings.

CHAPTER 11
Background Explanation

UNIT 1 A/V-(으)ㄴ/는데 ②

UNIT 2 A/V-(으)니까 ②

◎ What you'll learn in this chapter

Chapter 11 focuses on how to provide background explanations in Korean, particularly through two specific grammatical forms. This chapter enhances your conversations by enabling you to convey not just events, but also their broader contexts or underlying reasons. By the end of this chapter, your ability to communicate in Korean will be enriched with the skill to seamlessly combine explanations into your dialogues.

🎧 11-01G.mp3

한국어를 배우는데 어려워요.
I'm learning Korean, and it's difficult.

이 교실 진짜 큰데요.
This classroom is really spacious.

❶ A/V-(으)ㄴ/는데 [(eun)/neun·de]: background information

▶ -(으)ㄴ/는데 is used to introduce background information or set the context for what is mentioned in the following clause.

▶ This usage does not necessarily imply a contrastive meaning like the English 'but'.

▶ It's more about linking two related pieces of information, where the first part sets the stage for the second part.

한국 식당에 갔는데 음식이 정말 맛있었어요.
I went to a Korean restaurant, and the food was really delicious.

지 마드에 가는네 뭐 사올까요?
I'm going to the mart; what should I buy?

❷ A/V-(으)ㄴ/는데 as a Sentence-Ending

▶ -(으)ㄴ/는데 is also used as a sentence-ending form. In this role, it's used to express emotions like surprise or admiration.

A: 이 바지 어때요? How about these pants?
B: 아주 예쁜데요. They are very pretty.

→ 예쁜데요 indicates B's admiration or positive opinion about the pants.

▶ -(으)ㄴ/는데 is used to get a reaction or agreement from the listener.

A: 오늘 비가 너무 많이 오는데요. It's raining so much today.
B: 그럼 소풍은 내일 갈까요? Then, shall we go on the picnic tomorrow?

→ 오는데요 shows that the rain might affect their plans, hinting at the need for a new plan, which leads B to suggest a different day for the picnic.

✓
Rules of -(으)ㄴ/는데
Please refer to Unit 5 of Chapter 9 for the conjugation rules.

✓
-(으)ㄴ/는데 is used to present reasons for asking questions, making requests, proposing suggestions. Instead of directly revealing the reasons, it allows the listener to think by providing background explanations.
→ It is used to make suggestions more gently compared to -으니까.

오늘 날씨가 좋은데 같이 소풍 가요. The weather is nice, so let's go on a picnic together. (Explains the background for suggesting)

오늘 날씨가 좋으니까 같이 소풍 가요. Since the weather is nice, let's go on a picnic together. (Directly expresses the reason for suggesting)

Master Grammar By Practicing!

 11-01P.mp3

A Change the given word to complete the sentence, using '-(으)ㄴ/는데'.

있다 (to have)	→	내일 영어 시험이 <u>있는데</u> 몇 시에 시작해요?

1. 읽다 (to read) → 책을 _____ 좀 지루해요.

2. 아프다 (to be sick) → 고양이가 _____ 동물 병원에 갈까요?

3. 비슷하다 (to be similar) → 두 그림이 _____ 뭐가 더 좋아요?

4. 어리다 (to be young) → 동생이 _____ 한국어 수업 받을 수 있어요?

B Combine the two separate sentences into one sentence, using '-(으)ㄴ/는데'.

김치찌개가 없어요. 된장찌개를 드시겠어요? → <u>김치찌개가 없는데 된장찌개를 드시겠어요?</u>

1. 저는 열여덟 살이에요. 술 마실 수 있어요? → _____

2. 요즘 수영을 시작했어요. 매일 수영장에 가고 있어요. → _____

3. 언니는 남자친구가 있어요. 잘 생겼어요. → _____

4. 기분이 안 좋아. 영화 보러 갈까? → _____

C Choose the appropriate word and complete the conversation '-(으)ㄴ/는데'.

많다	깊다	없다	예쁘다	맛있다

A: 이 김밥 제가 만들었어요. 맛 보세요.   B: 김밥 정말 <u>맛있는데요</u>.

1. A: 수지 씨, 내일 같이 동물원 갈래요?   B: 저 내일 친구랑 약속 있어서 시간이 _____

2. A: 여기는 물이 너무 _____   B: 그럼 다른 곳으로 가서 수영할까요?

3. A: 어제 이 구두 샀어요. 어때요?   B: 색깔이 _____

4. A: 식당에 사람이 너무 _____   B: 조금만 기다리자.

🎧 11-02G.mp3

회사에 가니까 오늘 휴일이었어요.
When I went to the office,
I found out that today was a holiday.

하늘을 보니까 날씨가 맑아요.
I looked at the sky and saw
that the weather was clear.

❶ A/V-(으)니까 [(eu)·ni·kka] : when the fact discovered

▶ -(으)니까 is used not only for giving reasons but also for expressing a discovery or result. It links an action in the first clause to a newfound fact or situation revealed in the second clause.

▶ It implies that the speaker was not aware of the fact or situation in the second clause until after the action in the first clause was performed.

▶ It can be translated as 'when' or 'and find/discover'.

지갑을 여니까 돈이 하나도[1] 없었어요.
When I opened the wallet, there was no money at all.

김치를 먹으니까 그렇게[2] 맵지 않았어요.
When I ate the kimchi, it wasn't as spicy as I thought.

⚠ In this usage, -(으)니까 cannot be used with the past tense '-았/었'.

집에 돌아오니까 꽃 냄새가 났어요. (O)
When I returned home, there was a smell of flowers.

집에 돌아왔으니까 꽃 냄새가 났어요. (X)

✅ Rules of -(으)니까
Please refer to Unit 2 of Chapter 10 for the conjugation rules of verbs and adjectives.

[1] 하나도 is translated as 'not even one' or 'none at all' in English. It's used to emphasize the complete absence or lack of something.
돈이 하나도 없어요. There is not even a single penny.

[2] 그렇게 is translated as 'that much' or 'so'. It helps to compare or contrast the actual state of something against what was expected.
저는 K-POP을 그렇게 좋아하지 않아요.
I don't like K-POP that much.
요즘 그렇게 바빴어요?
Have you been that busy lately?

WORDS

휴일 [hyu·il] holiday　　하늘 [ha·neul] sky　　맑다 [malk·tta] to be clear
그렇다 [geu·reo·ta] to be like that　　냄새 [naem·sae] smell
나다 [na·da] to come out　　냄새가 나다 [naem·sae·ga na·da] to smell

Master Grammar By Practicing!

🎧 11-02P.mp3

A Choose the correct option.

> 아침에 (일어나니까 / 일어났니까) 벌써 열두 시였어요.

1. 서울에 (가으니까 / 가니까) 사람이 아주 많았어요.
2. 친구랑 (쇼핑하니까 / 쇼핑했으니까) 배가 너무 고팠어요.
3. 다리를 (건넜으니까 / 건너니까) 엄마가 기다리고 있었어요.
4. 의자에 (앉으니까 / 앉니까) 편했어요.

B Change the given word to complete the sentence, using '-(으)니까'.

> 쉬다 (to rest)　　　→　　　집에서 오래 <u>쉬니까</u> 이제 좀 심심해요.

1. 들어오다 (to come in)　→　집에 ＿＿＿＿＿＿＿＿부모님이 안 계셨어요.
2. 보다 (to see)　　　　→　거울을 ＿＿＿＿＿＿＿＿제 얼굴이 많이 늙었어요.
3. 되다 (to become)　　→　가을이 ＿＿＿＿＿＿＿＿날씨가 쌀쌀해요.
4. 섞다 (to mix)　　　　→　주스랑 커피를 ＿＿＿＿＿＿＿＿맛이 없어요.

C Choose the appropriate word and complete the conversation using '-(으)니까'.

입다　　　　기다리다　　　　보다　　　　타다　　　　전화하다

> A: 어제 일이 몇 시에 끝났어요?　　　　B: 시계 <u>보니까</u> 저녁 일곱 시였어요.

1. A: 서울에서 지하철을 ＿＿＿＿＿＿ 어땠어요?　B: 깨끗하고 편리했어요.
2. A: 그 옷 너무 작지 않아요?　　　　　B: ＿＿＿＿＿＿＿ 그렇게 작지 않아요.
3. A: 헨리한테 전화했어요?　　　　　　B: ＿＿＿＿＿＿＿ 헨리가 집에 없었어요.
4. A: 어제 소포 잘 받았어요?　　　　　B: 네, 한 시간 정도 ＿＿＿＿＿＿ 왔어요.

WORDS

다리 [da·ri] bridge　　**건너다** [geon·ne·da] to cross (over)　　**편하다** [pyeon·ha·da] to be comfortable
거울 [geo·ul] mirror　　**늙다** [neuk·tta] to become old　　**가을** [ga·eul] autumn
쌀쌀하다 [ssal·ssal·ha·da] to be chilly　　**섞다** [seok·tta] to mix
편리하다 [pyeol·li·ha·da] to be convenient

🎧 11-C.mp3

수지: 다니엘 씨, 오늘 날씨가 참 좋은데 같이 산책할까요?
Daniel, the weather is so nice today, shall we go for a walk together?

다니엘: 네, 좋아요. 공원에서 같이 걸어요.
Yes, that sounds great. Let's walk in the park together.

수지: 공원에 사람이 별로 없는데요.
There are not many people in the park, right?

다니엘: 네, 사람이 많지 않아서 조용해요.
Yes, there are not many people, so it's quiet.

그런데 밖에 나오니까 배가 고픈데요.
By the way, now that we've come out, I'm hungry.

수지: 저도 조금 배고픈데 점심 먹을래요?
I'm a bit hungry, too. Would you like to have lunch?

다니엘: 좋아요. 저기 저 식당 괜찮은데요.
Sure, that restaurant over there looks good.

수지: 저 식당 갈까요? Shall we go to that restaurant?

다니엘: 네, 저기에서 먹어요. Yes, let's eat there.

RECAP CHAPTER 11

❶ A/V-(으)ㄴ/는데: background information

Used to introduce background information or set the context for the following clause.

If the word is a verb → stem + 는데
If the word is an adjective, and it ends in a consonant → stem + 은데
If the word is an adjective, and it ends in a vowel → stem + ㄴ데
If the word is a 이다 → stem + ㄴ데 → 인데

❷ A/V-(으)ㄴ/는데요: sentence-ending form

1) Used to express emotions like surprise or admiration.
2) Used to get a reaction or agreement from the listener.

❸ A/V-(으)니까: when the fact discovered

Used to express a new discovery or result
In this usage, -(으)니까 cannot be used with the past tense

If the verb stem ends in a consonant → stem + 으니까
If the verb stem ends in a vowel → stem + 니까

REVIEW TEST CHAPTER 11

A Choose the correct option in the '-(으)ㄴ/는데요' form.

① 맛있다 - 맛있은데요   ② 멀다 - 먼데요

③ 흐리다 - 흐리는데요   ④ 고맙다 - 고맙은데요

B Choose the sentence where the underlined word is **incorrect**.

① 부엌에 가니까 김치 냄새가 났어요.

② 그 음식을 먹으니까 배가 아팠어요.

③ 한 시간 기다리니까 친구가 왔어요.

④ 상자를 열으니까 시계가 있었어요.

C Choose the correct arrangement of the words in brackets.

> I went to my friend's house yesterday, and there was a new sofa.
> (있었어요, 갔는데, 어제, 새 소파가, 친구 집에)

① 새 소파가 있었어요 어제 친구 집에 갔는데.

② 새 소파가 어제 갔는데 친구 집에 있었어요.

③ 어제 친구 집에 갔는데 새 소파가 있었어요.

④ 어제 친구 집에 새 소파가 갔는데 있었어요.

D In the following passage, choose the option that is written **incorrectly**.

> 어제 김치를 처음 ①만들었는데 쉽지 않았어요. 그런데 맛을 ②보니까 맛있었어요. 제 김치를 친구한테 ③주니까 아주 좋아했어요. 김치가 아직 ④많는데 가져가시겠어요?

E Choose the sentence that does **not** make sense.

① 과자를 구웠는데 드실래요?

② 시계를 보니까 밤 열 시였어요.

③ 요즘 한국어를 배우는데 맛있어요.

④ 회사에 가니까 일이 많았어요.

F Read the following dialogue and choose the **incorrect** statement.

> 제니: 요코 씨, 저 친구들이랑 한국어 스터디 하는데 같이 할래요?
> 요코: 너무 좋아요.
> 　　　모임이 언제예요?
> 제니: 수요일이랑 금요일이에요.
> 요코: 저 금요일에는 아르바이트 하는데요.
> 제니: 그럼 수요일에만 오세요.
> 요코: 달력 보니까 이번 주 금요일에는 일 안 해요. 이번 주에는 갈 수 있어요.
> 제니: 그럼 금요일에 봐요.

① 제니는 한국어 스터디 모임을 합니다.

② 스터디 모임은 일주일에 두 번 합니다.

③ 요코는 수요일에 아르바이트를 합니다.

④ 요코와 제니는 이번 주 금요일에 만납니다.

🎧 11-V.mp3

No.	✓	Word	Meaning
1	☐	그렇다	
2	☐	색깔	
3	☐	거울	
4	☐	잘생기다	
5	☐	냄새가 나다	
6	☐	섞다	
7	☐	건너다	
8	☐	맑다	
9	☐	어리다	
10	☐	깊다	
11	☐	쌀쌀하다	
12	☐	가을	
13	☐	비슷하다	
14	☐	하늘	
15	☐	냄새	
16	☐	색	
17	☐	늙다	
18	☐	동물원	
19	☐	편리하다	
20	☐	편하다	
21	☐	맛보다	
22	☐	맛	
23	☐	휴일	
24	☐	나다	
25	☐	다리	

Number of words I've learned: _____ / 25

Must-Know Korean Apps

When visiting Korea, it's evident that local apps are widely used over global apps like Google. These apps are indispensable for navigating daily life in Korea, providing convenience and accessibility to various services and goods. Here are some essential apps you should know:

카카오톡 KakaoTalk, 카카오 택시 Kakao Taxi

KakaoTalk, the largest messenger app in Korea, is widely used by smartphone users and often the first means of contact exchanged when meeting new friends. Kakao Taxi, beneficial for efficient transportation, is commonly used as hailing taxis on the street is rare.

네이버 Naver, 네이버맵 Naver Map

Naver, known as the 'green window', is Korea's largest search engine and integrates various services such as real-time news and weather updates. Naver Map offers comprehensive map features and services including real-time navigation and public transportation information.

쿠팡 Coupang

Coupang, the largest online marketplace in Korea, serves as a local substitute for global apps like Amazon. It offers same-day delivery, making shopping more convenient and often more affordable than offline stores.

배민 Baemin

Baemin, a leading food delivery service app, offers convenient and fast delivery of a wide variety of food options. Users can track their orders in real-time from payment to delivery, with choices ranging from traditional Korean cuisine to Western dishes and desserts.

당근 마켓 Carrot Market

Carrot Market, a mobile platform for buying and selling secondhand goods, operates on a location-based service allowing transactions within local communities. It ensures safe transactions by enabling users to evaluate and verify each other's reliability.

Unit 1 A/V-았/었다 (Past Tense) p. 11

A 1. 갔어요　　　　　　2. 그렸어요
　 3. 어려웠어요　　　　4. 여행했어요

B 1. 읽었어요.　　　　　2. 빌렸어요.
　 3. 재미없었어요.　　　4. 바쁘지 않았어요.

C 1. 추웠습니다 / 추웠어요 / 추웠어.
　 2. 깨끗했습니다 / 깨끗했어요 / 깨끗했어.
　 3. 받았습니다 / 받았어요 / 받았어.
　 4. 일어났습니다 / 일어났어요 / 일어났어.

Unit 2 Past Tense of 이다/아니다 p. 13

A 1. 박물관이었어요　　　2. 사람이었어
　 3. 휴가였어요　　　　　4. 배우였습니다

B 1. 의사였어요 / 의사가 아니었어요.
　 2. 사무실이었어요 / 사무실이 아니었어요.
　 3. 피아노였어요 / 피아노가 아니었어요.
　 4. 월요일이었어요 / 월요일이 아니었어요.

C 1. correct
　 2. incorrect, 대학교가 아니었어요.
　 3. incorrect, 방학이었습니다.
　 4. incorrect, 우산이 아니었어.

Unit 3 V-(으)ㄹ 것이다 ① (Future Tense) p. 15

A 1. 먹을 거야　　　　　2. 부를 거예요
　 3. 도울 거예요　　　　4. 갈 거예요

B 1. 초대할 거예요.　　　2. 쓸 거예요.
　 3. 바꿀 거예요.　　　　4. 살 거예요.

C 1. 퇴근할 것입니다 / 퇴근할 거예요 / 퇴근할 거야.
　 2. 찍을 것입니다 / 찍을 거예요 / 찍을 거야.
　 3. 탈 것입니다 / 탈 거예요 / 탈 거야.
　 4. 도울 것입니다 / 도울 거예요 / 도울 거야.

Unit 4 V-고 있다 (Progressive Tense) p. 17

A 1. 자고 있었어요　　　2. 요리하고 있어요
　 3. 읽고 있어요　　　　4. 보고 있었어요

B 1. 공부하고 있어요 / 공부하고 있었어요.
　 2. 놀고 있어요 / 놀고 있었어요.
　 3. 부르고 있어요 / 부르고 있었어요.
　 4. 먹고 있어요 / 먹고 있었어요.

C 1. incorrect, 타고 있어요.
　 2. correct
　 3. incorrect, 기다리고 있었어요?
　 4. incorrect, 듣고 있습니다.

REVIEW TEST p. 20

A　③ 춥다 - 춥웠어요 (→ 추웠어요)

B　① 이었어요 - 였어요

C　② 빌릴 거예요 - 들을 거예요.

D　③ 누구랑 같이 걸고 (→ 걷고) 있었어요?

E　① 만나었어요 (→ 만났어요)

F　③ 배우

G　④ (→ 수지는 내일 시간이 없습니다.)

VOCABULARY p. 21

1. (formal) shoes	2. Japan
3. yesterday	4. (a little) while ago
5. this time	6. to be clean
7. week	8. to pass by
9. hotel	10. vacation
11. auntie, ma'am	12. winter
13. red	14. university
15. hard, diligently	16. to live, to spend time
17. karaoke	18. to sleep
19. ski	20. to be boring
21. mister, sir	22. sneakers, sports shoes
23. office	24. last week
25. pants	26. to wear (shoes)
27. to invite	28. to change
29. to borrow	30. school vacation

31. gimbap (Korean rice roll) 32. next

33. sleep 34. last year

35. owner, proprietor 36. to play

37. the day before yesterday 38. dance

39. next year 40. blue

41. museum 42. to draw

43. auntie, ma'am 44. to take a photo

45. to dance 46. to leave work

47. kimchi stew 48. Vietnam

49. to dance 50. to wear (hat)

Chapter 2 Advanced Particles

Unit 1 N처럼, N같이 (like, as ... as) p. 25

A 1. 같이 2. 처럼
   3. 같이 4. 처럼

B 1. 산처럼 2. 아빠처럼
   3. 물처럼 4. 영화배우처럼

C 1. 따뜻해요. 2. 닮았어요.
   3. 아름다워요. 4. 친해요.

Unit 2 N마다 (every, all) p. 27

A 1. 오 분마다 2. 봄마다
   3. 금요일마다 4. 두 시간마다

B 1. 나라마다 2. 집집마다 (집마다)
   3. 계절마다 4. 학생마다

C 1. 매년 / 해마다 2. 매주 / 일주일마다
   3. 매월 / 달마다 4. 매일 / 날마다

Unit 3 N쯤, N 정도 (about, around) p. 29

A 1. 다섯 병쯤 2. 한 시쯤 (한 시쯤에)
   3. 내년 봄쯤 4. 열두 시간쯤

B 1. 두 잔 정도 2. 네 시간 정도
   3. 이만 원 정도 4. 일주일 정도

C 1. 다섯 시쯤 2. 마흔 살 정도
   3. 한 시간 정도 4. 만 원쯤

Unit 4 N밖에 (only, nothing but) p. 31

A 1. 안 샀어요 2. 못 해요
   3. 없어요 4. 안 왔어

B 1. 네 시간밖에 2. 케이팝밖에
   3. 핸드폰만 4. 김밥만

C 1. incorrect, 지우개만 2. incorrect, 우유밖에
   3. incorrect, 한 개밖에 4. correct

Unit 5 N(이)나 ② (as much as) p. 33

A 1. 이나 2. 이나
   3. 이나 4. 나

B 1. 세 잔이나 2. 두 시간이나
   3. 오만 원이나 4. 일곱 살이나

C 1. 스무 명이나 2. 열 시간이나
   3. 다섯 번이나 4. 여덟 권이나

Unit 6 N에게로, N에다가, N에서부터 p. 35

A 1. 벽에다가 2. 10(열) 시에서부터
   3. 종이에다가 4. 저에게로

B 1. 에다가 2. 에게로
   3. 에서부터 4. 에서부터

C 1. 에서부터 2. 에게로
   3. 에다가 4. 에서부터

REVIEW TEST p. 38

A ② 쯤

B ④ 저는 친구가 한 명밖에 없어요.

C ③ 이 모자는 삼만 원나 (→ 삼만 원이나) 해요.

D ④ 세 시간밖에 (→ 세 시간이나, 세 시간쯤, or 세 시간 정도)

E ③ 학교에서까지 (→ 학교까지 or 학교에서부터)

F ④ 이나 - 나

G ③ (→ 제니는 치마만 샀습니다.)

1. refrigerator   2. to place

3. to put, to add   4. season

5. pencil case   6. medicine

7. soccer   8. to end

9. customer   10. eraser

11. air conditioner   12. summer

13. candy   14. salt

15. to be bored   16. dining table

17. to laugh   18. culture

19. beauty salon   20. to do well, to be good (at)

21. soup   22. to be beautiful

23. how much   24. to come back

25. money   26. supermarket

27. spring   28. hometown

29. to become   30. to walk

31. to be a lot   32. class

33. to bring   34. to hang

35. cake   36. to be sweet

37. wallet   38. tennis

39. to hit, to play   40. meeting

41. to cry   42. game

43. day, a day   44. paper

45. homework   46. to be close (to someone)

47. to be late   48. won (Korean currency)

49. kilometer   50. orange

Chapter 3 Ability and Possibility

Unit 1 V-(으)ㄹ 수 있다/없다 (can/cannot)   p. 43

A 1. 올라갈 수 없어요   2. 쓸 수 있어요
   3. 읽을 수 있습니다   4. 닫을 수 없어?

B 1. 갈 수 있어요 / 갈 수 없어요.
   2. 지낼 수 있어요 / 지낼 수 없어요.
   3. 만들 수 있어요 / 만들 수 없어요.
   4. 씻을 수 있어요 / 씻을 수 없어요.

C 1. 쓸 수 있어요?   2. 보낼 수 있어요.
   3. 쓸 수 없었어요.   4. 팔 수 있어요.

Unit 2 V-(으)ㄹ 줄 알다/모르다   p. 45

A 1. 쓸 줄 압니다   2. 탈 줄 알아
   3. 먹을 줄 몰라요   4. 만들 줄 알아요?

B 1. 말할 줄 알아요 / 말할 줄 몰라요.
   2. 만들 줄 알아요 / 만들 줄 몰라요.
   3. 할 줄 알아요 / 할 줄 몰라요.
   4. 찍을 줄 알아요 / 찍을 줄 몰라요.

C 1. 담배를 피울 줄 몰라요.
   2. 고기를 구울 줄 몰라요.
   3. 중국어를 할 줄 알아요?
   4. 한복을 만들 줄 알아요.

REVIEW TEST   p. 48

A ① 갈 수 - 닫을 수

B ② 내가 너를 도울 수 있어.

C ③ 할 줄 알아요 - 구울 줄 알아요

D ② 물을 마실 수 없어요. (→ 없었어요)

E ④ 저는 축구를 할 줄 알아요. (→ 탁구를 칠 줄 알아요.)

F ② (→ It's not mentioned.)

VOCABULARY   p. 49

1. door   2. to use

3. item   4. traditional Korean clothing

5. internet	6. floor (level)
7. baseball	8. card
9. Hangul (Korean script)	10. already
11. washing machine	12. table tennis
13. embassy	14. to go up
15. to grill, to bake	16. writing
17. to smoke	18. bulgogi (Korean BBQ)
19. foreign language	20. to use
21. cigarette	22. foot

Chapter 4 Honorific Expressions

Unit 1 A/V-(으)시 (Honorific Suffix)   p. 53

A 1. 배우시다   2. 사시다   3. 씻으시다
   4. 구우시다   5. 받으시다   6. 슬프시다

B 1. 끄세요.   2. 괜찮으세요.
   3. 바꾸세요.   4. 사세요.

C 1. 꺼내십니다 / 꺼내세요 / 꺼내셔.
   2. 보십니다 / 보세요 / 보셔.
   3. 쓰십니다 / 쓰세요 / 쓰셔.
   4. 만드십니다 / 만드세요 / 만드셔.

Unit 2 N께서, N께서는, N께 (Honorific Particles) p. 55

A 1. 어머니께서는   2. 손님께
   3. 할아버지께서   4. 제니의 아버지께

B 1. 선생님께   2. 손님께서
   3. 삼촌께서는   4. 할머니께

C 1. 다니엘의 이모께서   2. 할아버지께
   3. 부모님께서   4. 사장님께서

Unit 3 Special Honorific Words   p. 57

A 1. 드셨어요?   2. 계세요.
   3. 드릴 거예요.   4. 주무세요?

B 1. 연세가   2. 드렸어요.
   3. 몇 분 계세요?   4. 할아버지께서는 말씀이

REVIEW TEST   p. 60

A ② 계세요 - 주무세요

B ③ 이름 - 성명 (→ 성함)

C ③ 할머니께 선물을 주었어요. (→ 드렸어요)

D ④ 아버지가 - 아버지께서

E ① 저분, 세요

F ② 살으세요 (→ 사세요)

G ③ (→ 연주가 교수님께 말씀드립니다.)

VOCABULARY   p. 61

1. professor	2. sometimes
3. key	4. program
5. to be little, to be few	6. menu
7. to turn off	8. pear
9. to take out	10. service
11. market	12. to order (food)
13. to die	14. beverage
15. ballpoint pen	16. rice cake
17. glass noodle dish	18. aunt
19. bowl	20. to explain
21. uncle	22. to be okay
23. fire	24. news
25. sports field	

Chapter 5 Imperatives and Requests

Unit 1 V-(으)세요 (do)   p. 65

A 1. 나가세요.   2. 켜세요.
   3. 쉬세요.   4. 입으세요.

B 1. 오십시오 / 오세요 / 와요 / 와.
   2. 닫으십시오 / 닫으세요 / 닫아요 / 닫아.

3. 갈아타십시오 / 갈아타세요 / 갈아타요 / 갈아타.

4. 읽으십시오 / 읽으세요 / 읽어요 / 읽어.

C 1. 여권을 가져오세요.   2. 택시를 타세요.

3. 편지를 보내세요.   4. 옷을 바꾸세요.

Unit 2 V-지 마세요 (do not)   p. 67

A 1. 운동하지 마십시오 / 운동하지 마세요 /
운동하지 마요 / 운동하지 마.

2. 올라오지 마십시오 / 올라오지 마세요 /
올라오지 마요 / 올라오지 마.

3. 닫지 마십시오 / 닫지 마세요 /
닫지 마요 / 닫지 마.

4. 사귀지 마십시오 / 사귀지 마세요 /
사귀지 마요 / 사귀지 마.

B 1. 전화하지 마세요.   2. 감지 마세요.

3. 들어가지 마세요.   4. 버리지 마세요.

C 1. 담배를 피우지 마세요.   2. 많이 걷지 마세요.

3. 구두를 신지 마세요.   4. 쇼핑을 하지 마세요.

Unit 3 V-아/어 주세요 (please do)   p. 69

A 1. 운전해 주세요.   2. 와 주세요.

3. 골라 주세요.   4. 꺼 주세요.

B 1. 불러 주십시오 / 불러 주세요 / 불러 줘요 / 불러 줘.

2. 앉아 주십시오 / 앉아 주세요 / 앉아 줘요 / 앉아 줘.

3. 기다려 주십시오 / 기다려 주세요 / 기다려 줘요 / 기다려 줘.

4. 씻어 주십시오 / 씻어 주세요 / 씻어 줘요 / 씻어 줘.

C 1. 도와 주세요.   2. 보여 주세요.

3. 찾아 주세요.   4. 바꿔 주세요.

REVIEW TEST   p. 72

A ③ 나가십시오 - 들으십시오

B ② 부모님을 도우세요.

C ③ 고기를 구지 (→ 굽지) 마세요.

D ④ A: 배가 아파 B: 담배를 피워 (→ 약을 먹어.)

E ② 알려 주세요 - 도와 주세요

F ④ (→ 다니엘이 제니에게 전화할 것입니다.)

VOCABULARY   p. 73

1. to lift, to carry   2. telephone number

3. for a moment   4. to find

5. elevator   6. later

7. to lie   8. to throw away

9. trash   10. face

11. to show   12. neck

13. bus stop   14. to go out

15. word   16. to inform

17. to answer   18. to come up

19. concert   20. to turn on

21. passport   22. to transfer (vehicles)

23. long (time)   24. leg

25. number   26. to close (eyes)

27. move (residence)   28. quickly

29. to be healthy   30. page

31. question   32. to be happy

33. towel   34. ticket

35. to date (someone)   36. black

37. taxi   38. to enter

39. eye   40. slowly

41. student ID

Chapter 6 Hope and Will

Unit 1 V-고 싶다 (I want)   p. 77

A 1. 쉬고 싶어요.   2. 사귀고 싶어요.

3. 살고 싶어요.   4. 운동하고 싶어요.

B 1. 초대하고 싶어해요   2. 씻고 싶어요

3. 듣고 싶어요?   4. 돌아가고 싶어했어요

C 1. 친구랑 이야기하고 싶어요.

2. 딸기를 먹고 싶어요.

3. 침대에 눕고 싶어했어요.

4. 케이크를 만들고 싶어요.

Unit 2 A/V-았/었으면 좋겠다 (I wish)   p. 79

A 1. 좋았으면 좋겠어요   2. 일어났으면 좋겠어요

3. 있었으면 좋겠어요   4. 가까웠으면 좋겠어요

B 1. 오면 좋겠어요 / 왔으면 좋겠어요.

2. 싸면 좋겠어요 / 쌌으면 좋겠어요.

3. 많으면 좋겠어요 / 많았으면 좋겠어요.

4. 읽으면 좋겠어요 / 읽었으면 좋겠어요.

C 1. 여자친구가 돌아왔으면 좋겠어요.

2. 일찍 잤으면 좋겠어요.

3. (몸이) 강했으면 좋겠어요.

4. 한국어를 잘했으면 좋겠어요.

Unit 3 V-(으)ㄹ래요 (I want)   p. 81

A 1. 살래요.   2. 먹을래요.

3. 살래요.   4. 넣을래요.

B 1. 이따가 먹을래요.   2. 차 마실래.

3. 집에서 쉴래요.   4. 흰색 티셔츠 살래.

C 1. 걸을래요?   2. 배울래요?

3. 만들래요?   4. 올라갈래요?

Unit 4 V-(으)ㄹ게요 (I will)   p. 83

A 1. 도와드릴게요.   2. 올게요.

3. 열게요.   4. 먹을게요.

B 1. 가져올 거예요?   2. 비쌀 거예요

3. 올 거예요.   4. 내려갈게요.

C 1.   사 줄게.   2. 닫을게요.

3. 올게요.   4. 물어볼게.

Unit 5 V-겠다 ① (I will)   p. 85

A 1. 끝내겠습니다.   2. 피우지 않겠습니다.

3. 데려오겠습니다.   4. 말씀드리겠습니다.

B 1. 공부하겠어요.   2. 약속을 지키겠어요.

3. 술을 마시지 않겠어요.   4. 일어나겠어요.

C 2. e   3. a

4. b   5. d

REVIEW TEST   p. 88

A ③ 집에 갈 수 있어요

B ④ 할래요 - 탈래요

C ② 집이 가깝웠으면 (→ 가까웠으면) 좋겠어요.

D ③ A: 배가 많이 고파요. B: 그럼 밥 먹지 마요.
      (→ 그럼 밥을 먹어요.)

E ④ 있으게요 (→ 있을게요)

F ③ 혼자 음악을 듣고 싶어요.

G ③ 수지는 김치찌개와 포도 (→ 사과) 주스를 골랐습니다.

VOCABULARY   p. 89

1. rain   2. alone

3. to return, to go back   4. dormitory

5. strawberry   6. certainly

7. parcel   8. to finish

9. to have, to possess   10. to start

11. gathering, meeting   12. to be bad (at)

13. to be weak   14. to go and come back

15. to blow   16. place

17. to bring someone   18. to leave

19. white   20. first

21. to talk, to tell a story   22. to hike

23. body   24. mandarin orange

25. (all of) you, everybody   26. to contact

27. chocolate   28. Thailand

29. tea   30. to keep (a promise)

31. ring   32. diet

33. half   34. plan

35. grape   36. to go down

37. to ask   38. to lie down

39. promise   40. to ask for a favor

41. city hall	42. t-shirt
43. to be slim	44. sugar
45. to be close	46. to be strong
47. wind	48. apartment
49. to sightsee	50. to prepare

Chapter 7 Making Suggestions

Unit 1 V-(으)ㅂ시다, V-아/어요, A/V-자 (let's) p. 93

A 1. 축하합시다.　　　　2. 먹읍시다.
　3. 탑시다.　　　　　　4. 달립시다.

B 1. 갑시다 / 가요 / 가자.
　2. 등산합시다 / 등산해요 / 등산하자.
　3. 만듭시다 / 만들어요 / 만들자.
　4. 출발합시다 / 출발해요 / 출발하자.

C 1. 타지 마요.　　　　　2. 헤어지지 말자.
　3. 들어가지 맙시다.　　4. 마시지 말자.

Unit 2 V-(으)ㄹ까요? (shall we/I?) p. 95

A 1. 시킬까요?　　　　　2. 탈까요, 탈까요?
　3. 걸을까요?　　　　　4. 여행갈까요?

B 1. 내릴까요?　　　　　2. 입을까요?
　3. 드릴까요?　　　　　4. 건너갈까요?

C 1. 살까요?　　　　　　2. 놓을까요?
　3. 걸까요?　　　　　　4. 만날까요?

Unit 3 V-(으)시겠어요? (would you like to?) p. 97

A 1. 쉬시겠어요?　　　　2. 오시겠어요?
　3. 갈아입으시겠어요?　4. 감으시겠어요?

B 1. 쓰시겠어요?　　　　2. 신으시겠어요?
　3. 말하시겠어요?　　　4. 쉬시겠어요?

C 1. 씻으시겠어요?　　　2. 사시겠어요?
　3. 가르쳐 주시겠어요?　4. 보시겠어요?

REVIEW TEST p. 100

A ③ 다 같이 사진 찍을까?

B ④ 건너갈까요?

C ③ 운동화를 신시겠어요? (→ 신으시겠어요?)

D ② A: 이 떡 좀 드시겠어요? B: 네, 떡을 드릴까요?
　　(→ 네, 떡을 먹을게요.)

E ② 가웁시다 (→ 갑시다)

F ① 마시자 - 앉자

G ④ 지수가 (→ 유나가) 물건을 가져올 것입니다.

VOCABULARY p. 101

1. stamp	2. watermelon
3. wall	4. persimmon
5. date	6. to take
7. a moment	8. luggage
9. picnic	10. to go across
11. opposite side	12. beer
13. to decide	14. to part, to break up
15. travel agency	16. to change clothes
17. to run	18. all, everything
19. seat, place	20. to congratulate
21. ribs	22. address
23. marriage	24. first
25. reason	26. ship
27. now	28. building
29. soybean paste stew	30. this way, this side
31. purple	32. Incheon
33. to get off, to unload	34. to cut
35. radio	36. hair
37. to depart	38. hand
39. to have a meal	40. everyone, everything
41. station	

Unit 1 V-(으)러 가다/오다 (to go/come to)   p. 105

A 1. 낚시하러   2. 도우러
   3. 인사하러   4. 팔러

B 1. 보러 미술관에 가요.   2. 사러 꽃집에 갔어.
   3. 타러 스키장에 갔어요.   4. 사러 마트에 가.

C 2. d → 타러   마. 기차역에 가요.
   3. a → 사러,   다. 빵집에 가요.
   4. e → 먹으러   라. 식당에 가요.
   5. b → 찾으러   가. 은행에 가요.

Unit 2 V-(으)려고 (in order to)   p. 107

A 1. 쉬려고   2. 찾아보려고
   3. 고치려고   4. 씻으려고

B 1. 배우려고 (책을) 읽어요.
   2. 같이 먹으려고 (케이크를) 만들었어요.
   3. 알려 주려고 전화했어요.
   4. 사려고 (마트에) 들렀어요.

C 1. correct   2. incorrect, 공부하려고
   3. incorrect, 먹으러   4. correct

Unit 3 V-(으)려고 하다, V-기로 하다   p. 109

A 1. 일하려고 해요.   2. 걸으려고 해요.
   3. 쉬려고 해요.   4. 버리려고 해요.

B 1. 끊기로 했어요.   2. 가져오기로 했어요.
   3. 쓰기로 했어요.   4. 예약하기로 했어요.

C 1. 여행가려고   2. 잊기로
   3. 시작하기로   4. 바꾸려고

Unit 4 V-게 (so that)   p. 111

A 1. 주문하게   2. 넘어지지 않게
   3. 따뜻하게   4. 사게

B 1. 볼 수 있게   2. 앉을 수 있게
   3. 먹을 수 있게   4. 끊을 수 있게

C 1. 연필을 쓰게 깎아주세요.
   2. 살을 뺄 수 있게 헬스클럽에 다녀요.

3. 실수하지 않게 열심히 준비하세요.
4. 잘 볼 수 있게 불을 켜 주세요.

REVIEW TEST   p. 114

A ② 끊으려고 - 빼려고

B ② 한국어를 배우려고 (→ 배우게) 책을 주세요.

C ② 그림을 보러 (→ 운동하러) 헬스클럽에 갔어요.

D ③ 배우려고 - 다니기로

E ① 축하할려고 (→ 축하하려고)

F ① 10층에 가려고 엘리베이터를 탔어요.

G ④ (→ 제니는 민호의 생일을 다음에 축하할 것입니다.)

VOCABULARY   p. 115

1. to chew   2. to quit
3. lake   4. mart
5. to fish   6. beef
7. to be careful   8. soon
9. dictionary   10. snack
11. far away   2. major (field of study)
13. to forget   14. to pass by
15. to fall down   16. diary
17. to look up, to search   18. to go on a date
19. New Year   20. to gather
21. ski resort   22. again
23. flower shop   24. red chili paste
25. graduation   26. to repair
27. to come down   28. in advance
29. quietly   30. gym, health club
31. bakery   32. train station
33. cook, chef   34. to reserve
35. to clean, to polish   36. just (now)
37. to remove, to lose weight 38. to make a mistake

39. history
40. restroom
41. to order (items or food)
42. art gallery
43. to greet
44. fat
45. private academy
46. to stop by
47. to worry
48. to grab, to catch
49. to peel, to cut
50. gum

Chapter 9 Connecting Sentences

Unit 1 A/V-고 (and) p. 119

A 1. 맵고   2. 학생이고
3. 빌리고   4. 초대하고

B 1. 이 음식은 맵고 짜요.
2. 저는 영화를 보고 제니는 탁구를 쳤어요.
3. 엄마는 선생님이고 아빠는 경찰이에요.
4. 저는 일본에 가고 언니는 캐나다에 갔어요.

C 1. 테니스를 치고 집에서 쉴 거예요.
2. 공부하고 편의점에 갈 거예요.
3. 커피를 마시고 신문을 읽을 거예요.
4. 이메일을 보내고 노래를 연습할 거예요.

Unit 2 V-아/어서 ① (and then) p. 121

A 1. 만들어서   2. 일어나서
3. 들어서   4. 골라서

B 1. 지하철역에 가서 지하철을 탈 거예요.
2. 선물을 사서 제니한테 줄 거예요.
3. 일찍 일어나서 운동할 거예요.
4. 사과를 씻어서 먹을 거예요.

C 1. 가서   2. 먹고
3. 사고   4. 사서

Unit 3 A/V-거나 (or) p. 123

A 1. 타거나   2. 자거나
3. 그리거나   4. 하거나

B 1. 주말에 외국어를 배우거나 축구를 해요.
2. 파티에서 노래를 부르거나 춤을 출 거예요.

3. 약국에서 감기약을 사거나 병원에 갈 거예요.
4. 일요일에 청소를 하거나 빨래를 할 거예요.

C 1. 영화나 연극을   2. 테니스나 탁구를
3. 시계나 달력을   4. 1(일)월이나 2(이)월에

Unit 4 A/V-지만 (but, however) p. 125

A 1. 신지만   2. 찍지만
3. 재미없지만   4. 짜지만

B 1. 보려고 했지만   2. 바빴지만
3. 재미있지만   4. 졸업했지만

C 1. 한국 음식을 좋아하지만 아직 젓가락을 못 써요.
2. 요리를 자주 하지만 제 음식은 맛없어요.
3. 배가 아팠지만 병원에 가지 않았어요.
4. 공항에 갔지만 친구를 못 만났어요.

Unit 5 A/V-(으)ㄴ/는데 ① (but) p. 127

A 1. 주말인데   2. 봤는데
3. 많은데   4. 매운데

B 1. incorrect, 맛있는데   2. incorrect, 큰데
3. correct   4. incorrect, 겨울인데

C 1. 점심을 많이 먹었는데 배가 고파요.
2. 화요일마다 피아노를 배우는데 잘 못 쳐요.
3. 이 물건은 가격이 비싼데 별로 안 좋아요.
4. 저는 인도네시아 사람인데 한국어를 잘해요.

REVIEW TEST p. 130

A ③ 입고 - 씻어서

B ② 영화를 볼거나 (→ 보거나) 운동을 할 거예요.

C ① 맛있는데 - 예쁜데

D ② 갔어서 (→ 가서)

E ③ 열심히 공부하지만 (→ 공부했지만) 시험을 못 봤어요.

F ② 지만

G ③ (→ 헨리는 아침을 먹고 산에 갑니다.)

VOCABULARY

p. 131

1. still, yet	2. to be boring
3. hamburger	4. subway
5. subway station	6. stomach
7. price	8. lover
9. really, truly	10. to be famous
11. basketball	12. new
13. to be sour	14. movie theater
15. to not be delicious	16. watch, clock
17. nurse	18. calendar
19. to be salty	20. to be tired
21. pharmacy	22. continuously
23. to be bitter	24. post office
25. spaghetti	26. to be smart
27. pizza	28. chopsticks
29. not much, not really	30. to be quiet
31. to take a walk	32. just, simply
33. to practice	34. mood
35. university	36. newspaper
37. Canada	38. necklace
39. swimming pool	40. convenience store
41. airport	42. sofa
43. play (theater)	44. Indonesia
45. to do laundry	46. furniture
47. cosmetics	48. police
49. cold (illness)	50. cold noodles

Chapter 10 — Causes and Reasons

Unit 1 A/V-아/어서 ② (because)

p. 135

A 1. 재미있어서   2. 거짓말해서
   3. 걸어서   4. 어려워서

B 1. 길을 몰라서 지도를 봤어요.
   2. 요즘 외로워서 남자친구를 사귀고 싶어요.
   3. 내일이 친구 생일이어서(생일이라서) 파티를 할 거예요.
   4. 비가 와서 우산을 샀어요.

C 1. 싸워서   2. 잃어버려서
   3. 많아서   4. 지루해서

Unit 2 A/V-(으)니까 ① (because)

p. 137

A 1. 더러우니까   2. 시험 보니까
   3. 맛있으니까   4. 시간이 없으니까

B 1. 손님이 오니까 청소를 해요.
   2. 얼음이 진짜 차가우니까 조심하세요.
   3. 방이 어두우니까 불을 켜 주세요.
   4. 그 영화 무서우니까 놀라지 마세요.

C 1. 시끄러우니까   2. 뜨거우니까
   3. 도와주셔서   4. 늦어서

Unit 3 N 때문에, A/V-기 때문에

p. 139

A 1. 재미있기 때문에   2. 태어나기 때문에
   3. 젊기 때문에   4. 키우기 때문에

B 1. 싸기 때문에   2. 살기 때문에
   3. 좋아하기 때문에   4. 한국 사람이기 때문에

C 1. 날씨 때문에   2. 외웠기 때문에
   3. 많으니까   4. 아르바이트 때문에

REVIEW TEST

p. 142

A ① 아파서 - 피워서

B ③ 일을 많이 했기 때문에 조금 피곤해요.

C ② 제 친구는 신발을 사고 싶어서 가게에 갔어요.

D ④ 하기 때문에 (→ 했기 때문에 or 해서)

E ② 저를 도와주니까 (→ 도와줘서) 고마워요.

F ④ 케이크가 써서 맛있었어요. (→ 맛없었어요)

G ③ (→ 지수는 다이어트 때문에 저녁을 안 먹습니다.)

VOCABULARY p. 143

1. to be glad	2. animal
3. again	4. to be born
5. to fight	6. snow
7. anger	8. to be cold
9. finger	10. to be hot
11. to be dark	12. to be surprised
13. to be hurt	14. to get well
15. to cancel	16. mosquito
17. to be pitiful	18. so, therefore
19. sandwich	20. to be lonely
21. to be scary	22. to be dirty
23. to be angry	24. to be necessary
25. foreign country	26. map
27. to be noisy	28. rich person
29. popularity	30. to lose (something)
31. ice	32. to go to work
33. to raise, to grow	34. to memorize
35. to be kind	36. mistake, wrong
37. soy sauce	38. toe
39. to be young	

Chapter 11 Background Explanation

Unit 1 A/V-(으)ㄴ/는데 ② p. 147

A 1. 읽는데   2. 아픈데
   3. 비슷한데   4. 어린데

B 1. 저는 열여덟 살인데 술 마실 수 있어요?
   2. 요즘 수영을 시작했는데 매일 수영장에 가고 있어요.
   3. 언니는 남자친구가 있는데 잘 생겼어요.
   4. 기분이 안 좋은데 영화 보러 갈까?

C 1. 없는데요   2. 깊은데요.
   3. 예쁜데요.   4. 많은데.

Unit 2 A/V-(으)니까 ② p. 149

A 1. 가니까   2. 쇼핑하니까
   3. 건너니까   4. 앉으니까

B 1. 들어오니까   2. 보니까
   3. 되니까   4. 섞으니까

C 1. 타니까   2. 입으니까
   3. 전화하니까   4. 기다리니까

REVIEW TEST p. 152

A ② 멀다 - 먼데요

B ④ 상자를 열으니까 (→ 여니까) 시계가 있었어요.

C ③ 어제 친구 집에 갔는데 새 소파가 있었어요.

D ④ 많는데 (→ 많은데)

E ③ 요즘 한국어를 배우는데 멋있어요. (→ 재미있어요.)

F ③ 요코는 수요일에(→ 금요일에) 아르바이트를 합니다.

VOCABULARY p. 153

1. to be like that	2. color
3. mirror	4. to be good-looking
5. to smell	6. to mix
7. to cross (over)	8. to be clear
9. to be young	10. to be deep
11. to be chilly	12. autumn
13. to be similar	14. sky
15. smell	16. color
17. to become old	18. zoo
19. to be convenient	20. to be comfortable
21. to taste, to try	22. taste
23. holiday	24. to come out
25. bridge	

Index of Grammar

Index of Vocabulary

드시다	honorific to eat	Ch. 4
들다	to lift, to carry	Ch. 5
들르다	to stop by	Ch. 8
들어가다	to enter	Ch. 5
등산하다	to hike	Ch. 6
딸기	strawberry	Ch. 6
떠나다	to leave	Ch. 6
떡	rice cake	Ch. 4
또	again	Ch. 8
똑똑하다	to be smart	Ch. 9
뜨겁다	to be hot	Ch. 10

ㄹ

라디오	radio	Ch. 7

ㅁ

마트	mart	Ch. 8
많다	to be a lot	Ch. 2
만다	to stop, to not do	Ch. 5
말씀	honorific words	Ch. 4
맑다	to be clear	Ch. 11
맛	taste	Ch. 11
맛보다	to taste, to try	Ch. 11
맛없다	to not be delicious	Ch. 9
매년	annually, every year	Ch. 1
매달	monthly, every month	Ch. 1
매주	weekly, every week	Ch. 1
맥주	beer	Ch. 7
머리카락	hair	Ch. 7
먼저	first	Ch. 7
멀리	far away	Ch. 8
메뉴	menu	Ch. 4
모기	mosquito	Ch. 10
모두	everyone, everything	Ch. 7
모으다	to gather	Ch. 8
모임	gathering, meeting	Ch. 6

목	neck	Ch. 5
목걸이	necklace	Ch. 9
몸	body	Ch. 6
못하다	to be bad (at)	Ch. 6
무섭다	to be scary	Ch. 10
문	door	Ch. 3
문화	culture	Ch. 2
물건	item	Ch. 3
물어보다	to ask	Ch. 6
미리	in advance	Ch. 8
미술관	art gallery	Ch. 8
미용실	beauty salon	Ch. 2

ㅂ

바꾸다	to change	Ch. 1
바람	wind	Ch. 6
바지	pants	Ch. 1
박물관	museum	Ch. 1
반	class	Ch. 2
반	half	Ch. 6
반지	ring	Ch. 6
발	foot	Ch. 3
발가락	toe	Ch. 10
방금	just (now)	Ch. 8
방학	school vacation	Ch. 1
배	pear	Ch. 4
배	ship	Ch. 7
배	stomach	Ch. 9
버리다	to throw away	Ch. 5
번	time	Ch. 1
번호	number	Ch. 5
벌써	already	Ch. 3
베트남	Vietnam	Ch. 1
벽	wall	Ch. 7
별로	not much, not really	Ch. 9
보라색	purple	Ch. 7

쌀쌀하다	to be chilly	Ch. 11
쓰다	to wear (hat)	Ch. 1
쓰다	to use	Ch. 3
쓰다	to be bitter	Ch. 9
쓰레기	trash	Ch. 5
씹다	to chew	Ch. 8

ㅇ

아까	a (little) while ago	Ch. 1
아름답다	to be beautiful	Ch. 2
아저씨	mister, sir	Ch. 1
아주머니	auntie, ma'am	Ch. 1
아줌마	auntie, ma'am	Ch. 1
아직	still, yet	Ch. 9
아파트	apartment	Ch. 6
알리다	to inform	Ch. 5
애인	lover	Ch. 9
야구	baseball	Ch. 3
약	medicine	Ch. 2
약국	pharmacy	Ch. 9
약속	promise	Ch. 6
약하다	to be weak	Ch. 6
어둡다	to be dark	Ch. 10
어리다	to be young	Ch. 11
어제	yesterday	Ch. 1
얼굴	face	Ch. 5
얼마	how much	Ch. 2
얼음	ice	Ch. 10
에어컨	air conditioner	Ch. 2
엘리베이터	elevator	Ch. 5
여권	passport	Ch. 5
여러분	(all of) you, everybody	Ch. 6
여름	summer	Ch. 2
여쭙다	honorific to ask	Ch. 4
여행사	travel agency	Ch. 7
역	station	Ch. 7

역사	history	Ch. 8
연극	play (theater)	Ch. 9
연락하다	to contact	Ch. 6
연세	honorific age	Ch. 4
연습하다	to practice	Ch. 9
열쇠	key	Ch. 4
열심히	hard, diligently	Ch. 1
영화관	movie theater	Ch. 9
예약하다	to reserve	Ch. 8
오래	long (time)	Ch. 5
오렌지	orange	Ch. 2
올라가다	to go up	Ch. 3
올라오다	to come up	Ch. 5
왜	why	Ch. 8
외국	foreign country	Ch. 10
외국어	foreign language	Ch. 3
외롭다	to be lonely	Ch. 10
외우다	to memorize	Ch. 10
요리사	cook, chef	Ch. 8
우체국	post office	Ch. 9
우표	stamp	Ch. 7
운동장	sports field	Ch. 4
운동화	sneakers, sports shoes	Ch. 1
울다	to cry	Ch. 2
웃다	to laugh	Ch. 2
원	won (Korean currency)	Ch. 2
유명하다	to be famous	Ch. 9
음료수	beverage	Ch. 4
이따가	later	Ch. 5
이모	aunt	Ch. 4
이번	this time	Ch. 1
이사	move (residence)	Ch. 5
이야기하다	to talk, to tell a story	Ch. 6
이유	reason	Ch. 7
이제	now	Ch. 7
이쪽	this way, this side	Ch. 7

인기	popularity	Ch. 10
인도네시아	Indonesia	Ch. 9
인사하다	to greet	Ch. 8
인천	Incheon	Ch. 7
인터넷	internet	Ch. 3
일기	diary	Ch. 8
일본	Japan	Ch. 1
일주일	a week	Ch. 1
잃어버리다	to lose (something)	Ch. 10
잊다	to forget	Ch. 8

ㅈ

자르다	to cut	Ch. 7
자리	seat, place	Ch. 7
작년	last year	Ch. 1
잘못	mistake, wrong	Ch. 10
잘생기다	to be good-looking	Ch. 11
잘하다	to be good (at)	Ch. 2
잠	sleep	Ch. 1
잠깐	a moment	Ch. 7
잠시	for a moment	Ch. 5
잠자다	to sleep	Ch. 1
잡다	to grab, to catch	Ch. 8
잡수시다	honorific to eat	Ch. 4
잡채	glass noodle dish	Ch. 4
장소	place	Ch. 6
재미없다	to be boring	Ch. 1
적다	to be little, to be few	Ch. 4
전공	major (field of study)	Ch. 8
전화번호	telephone number	Ch. 5
젊다	to be young	Ch. 10
젓가락	chopsticks	Ch. 9
정류장	bus stop	Ch. 5
정하다	to decide	Ch. 7
조심하다	to be careful	Ch. 8
조용하다	to be quiet	Ch. 9

조용히	quietly	Ch. 8
졸업	graduation	Ch. 8
좀	a little, somewhat	Ch. 5
종이	paper	Ch. 2
주	week	Ch. 1
주무시다	honorific to sleep	Ch. 4
주문하다	to order (items or food)	Ch. 8
주소	address	Ch. 7
주인	owner, proprietor	Ch. 1
죽다	to die	Ch. 4
준비하다	to prepare	Ch. 6
지갑	wallet	Ch. 2
지나가다	to pass by	Ch. 8
지나다	to pass by	Ch. 1
지난달	last month	Ch. 1
지난해	last year	Ch. 1
지난주	last week	Ch. 1
지내다	to live, to spend time	Ch. 1
지도	map	Ch. 10
지루하다	to be boring	Ch. 9
지우개	eraser	Ch. 2
지키다	to keep (a promise)	Ch. 6
지하철	subway	Ch. 9
지하철역	subway station	Ch. 9
진지	honorific meal	Ch. 4
질문	question	Ch. 5
짐	luggage	Ch. 7
짜다	to be salty	Ch. 9
쪽	page	Ch. 5
찍다	to take a photo, to film	Ch. 1

ㅊ

차	tea	Ch. 6
차갑다	to be cold	Ch. 10
참	really, truly	Ch. 9
찾다	to find	Ch. 5

찾아보다	to look up, to search	Ch. 8
처음	first	Ch. 6
천천히	slowly	Ch. 5
초대하다	to invite	Ch. 1
초콜릿	chocolate	Ch. 6
추다	to dance	Ch. 1
축구	soccer	Ch. 2
축하하다	to congratulate	Ch. 7
출근하다	to go to work	Ch. 10
출발하다	to depart	Ch. 7
춤	dance	Ch. 1
춤추다	to dance	Ch. 1
취소하다	to cancel	Ch. 10
층	floor (level)	Ch. 3
치다	to hit, to play	Ch. 2
친절하다	to be kind	Ch. 10
친하다	to be close (to someone)	Ch. 2

ㅋ

카드	card	Ch. 3
캐나다	Canada	Ch. 9
케이크	cake	Ch. 2
켜다	to turn on	Ch. 5
콘서트	concert	Ch. 5
키우다	to raise, to grow	Ch. 10
킬로미터	kilometer	Ch. 2

ㅌ

탁구	table tennis	Ch. 3
태국	Thailand	Ch. 6
태어나다	to be born	Ch. 10
택시	taxi	Ch. 5
테니스	tennis	Ch. 2
퇴근하다	to leave work	Ch. 1
티셔츠	t-shirt	Ch. 6

ㅍ

파란색	blue	Ch. 1
편리하다	to be convenient	Ch. 11
편의점	convenience store	Ch. 9
편하다	to be comfortable	Ch. 11
포도	grape	Ch. 6
표	ticket	Ch. 5
프로그램	program	Ch. 4
피곤하다	to be tired	Ch. 9
피우다	to smoke	Ch. 3
피자	pizza	Ch. 9
필요하다	to be necessary	Ch. 10
필통	pencil case	Ch. 2

ㅎ

하늘	sky	Ch. 11
하루	day, a day	Ch. 2
학생증	student ID	Ch. 5
학원	private academy	Ch. 8
한글	Hangul (Korean script)	Ch. 3
한복	traditional Korean clothing	Ch. 3
햄버거	hamburger	Ch. 9
행복하다	to be happy	Ch. 5
헤어지다	to part, to break up	Ch. 7
헬스클럽	gym, health club	Ch. 8
호수	lake	Ch. 8
호텔	hotel	Ch. 1
혼자	alone	Ch. 6
화	anger	Ch. 10
화나다	to be angry	Ch. 10
화장실	restroom	Ch. 8
화장품	cosmetics	Ch. 9
회의	meeting	Ch. 2
휴가	vacation	Ch. 1
휴일	holiday	Ch. 11
흰색	white	Ch. 6

About the Author

Tomi (Lee Insuk):
Tomi was born and raised in Seoul, South Korea, and currently resides in Germany. In Korea, she studied Korean history at Sungkyunkwan University, the oldest university in Korea. Working as an editor for the Korean cultural magazine <PAPER>, she also engaged in scriptwriting for Korean broadcasters such as MBC and MTV.

After immigrating to Germany, Tomi began teaching Korean to foreign students. For several years, she worked as a Korean language teacher at the Bremen Korean School and Inlingua language school. With a dream of making Korean language learning easier and more enjoyable for learners worldwide, she actively participates on Instagram and YouTube.

Instagram: @tomikorean
YouTube Channel: @tomikoren
Website: www.tomikorean.com

Contributors to Production:
Text: Hwang Bora
Media: Jung Sanghoon

Your Opinion Counts!

We sincerely hope this book has been a valuable
resource in your Korean language learning journey.

If you've found it helpful, please take a moment to
leave a review on our website or Amazon
to help other Korean learners discover it.
We would greatly appreciate your review!

Thank you so much!

Made in the USA
Monee, IL
09 August 2024

63560905R00098